Stop Motion

Focal Press Visual Effects and Animation

Debra Kaufman, Series Editor

Stop Motion

Craft skills for model animation

Susannah Shaw

Modelmaking and animation sequences
created and photographed by
Cat Russ and Gary Jackson, ScaryCat Studio

Illustrations
Tony Guy and Susannah Shaw

AMSTERDAM • BOSTON • HEIDELBERG • LONDON • NEW YORK • OXFORD
PARIS • SAN DIEGO • SAN FRANCISCO • SINGAPORE • SYDNEY • TOKYO
Focal Press is an imprint of Elsevier

ELSEVIER

Focal
Press

Focal Press
An imprint of Elsevier
Linacre House, Jordan Hill, Oxford OX2 8DP
30 Corporate Drive, Burlington, MA 01803

First published 2004
Reprinted 2005

British Library Cataloguing in Publication Data
A catalogue record for this book is available from the British Library

Library of Congress Cataloguing in Publication Data
A catalogue record for this book is available from the Library of Congress

ISBN 0 240 51659 1

Please note that although some brand names have been included for ease of
communications, no endorsement is intended by this inclusion and no discredit is
intended by omission

For information on all Focal Press publications
visit our website at www.focalpress.com

Working together to grow
libraries in developing countries

www.elsevier.com | www.bookaid.org | www.sabre.org

ELSEVIER   BOOK AID
            International   Sabre Foundation

Printed and bound in Italy by Printer Trento

dedication

This book is dedicated to Bob Godfrey, whose book *Do It Yourself Film Animation* inspired so many people to get started.

contents

acknowledgements

Thanks to Gary Jackson & Cat Russ of ScaryCat Studio; Tony Guy; Ian Mackinnonn, Peter Saunders & Christine Walker of Mackinnon & Saunders; Barry Purves; Jeff Newitt; Guionne Leroy; Timothy Hittle; Sara Mullock; Helen Nabarro at the BBC Animation Unit; Nick Hilligoss at ABC; Ange Palethorpe, Glen Holberton and Emma Bruce at Loose Moose; John Schofield at bolexbrothers; Blair Clark at Tippett Studios; Lionel Orozco of Stop Motion Works; David McCormick; Helen Garrard; Tristan Oliver; Bob Thorne at Artem; Anthony Scott; Trey Thomas; Richard Goleszowski; John Wright at John Wright Modelmaking; Miguel Grinberg (MagPie); Brigid Appleby & Mark Hall of Cosgrove Hall; Jackie Cockle & Sarah Ball of Hot Animation; Barry Bruce at Vinton's; Nigel Cornford; James Mather; John Parsons; Pete Lord, Helen Brunsdon, Luis Cook, Nick Park, Sharron Traer, Dave Sproxton, Dan Lane, Tom Barnes, Jan Sanger, Martin Shann, Ian Fleming, & Michael Carter of Aardman Animations; Chris Webster at UWE; Rick Catizone; Chris Grace at S4C; Jack and Elke Counsell, and for keeping me on track: Loyd Price at Aardman. Last of all: Ken, Kitty and Alice for their patience.

elements of an animation shoot

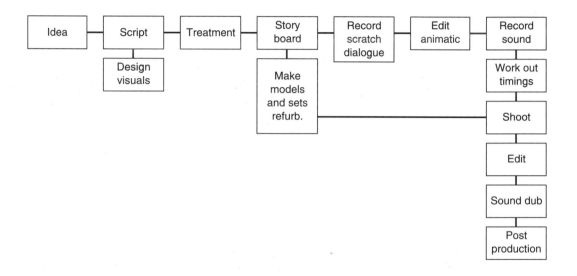

chapter 1

introduction – playing God

chapter summary	• nature and caricature • what this book is for

> *You want to captivate people. It doesn't come with just technique, it's about putting yourself inside that character. It's like slowing down your brain and all of a sudden you are that puppet and you move how that puppet moves.*
> Guionne Leroy – animator on *Chicken Run*, *Toy Story*, *James and the Giant Peach*

If you want to make great animation, you need to know how to control a whole world: how to make a character, how to make that character live and be happy or sad. You need to create four walls around them, a landscape, the sun and moon – a whole life for them. But it's not just playing dolls – it's more like playing God. You have to get inside that puppet and first make it live, then make it *perform*.

Animation is animation, whatever the medium. Whether you are drawing on paper, modelling in Plasticine, shoving a couple of matchboxes around in front of a Bolex camera or animating with a computer; to become an animator you will need to understand movement and how to create emotion. You can be a cartoonist or an artist on film, a moving image-maker, and there are many beautiful and hilarious examples of this, but they do not necessarily fulfil the definition of animation that this book sets out to demonstrate. This book is written for someone wanting to take the first steps in creating three-dimensional character animation.

Methods for 2D animation have been documented for a long time. Since the formation of the Disney Studios, their vast commercial output meant they had to find ways of passing on their skills to a large body of workers who needed to know the house 'style'. The top animators started to look at what they were doing as animators and started to identify 'rules' and guiding principles by which they worked. Most of these principles apply to model or puppet animation as well as – as they are derived from the scientific study of movement – the effect of gravity, friction and force on masses. One of the greatest books to read about the development of 2D animation is Ollie Johnston and Frank Thomas's *The Illusion of Life* (1997).

You will have seen computer animation that seems wooden and stiff or the characters glide and swoop about as though gravity never existed. This is simply because, in this new medium, the majority of practitioners were originally from a computing background and have learned the computing skills but not necessarily the animating skills. Director John Lasseter was a successful 2D animator before applying his skills to the computer-generated *Tin Toy, Knick Knack*, and more famously, *Toy Story* and *Monsters Inc.*, giving Pixar some of the best computer-generated characters seen so far. Not everyone can handle both skills that well.

In Europe and Asia, model animation has grown out of a tradition of storytelling, fable and legend. Most practitioners developed their own ways of working in isolation, many re-inventing the wheel, but in very few cases were methods documented, and certainly no 'principles' for model animation had been laid down in the same way as for 2D. But the basic laws of movement apply to any form of animation.

For many years Eastern Europe was the source of puppet animation, in the US the film experimentation settled more quickly to making 2D drawn animation. But in Eastern Europe there was a long tradition of puppeteering; for some film was seen as a natural medium for the art. Puppeteers had to be able to breathe life into a jointed wooden doll in very much the same way as animators do. The design element of the puppet was very important to the storytelling process – they would need to communicate a character over a distance to the whole audience. Jiri Trnka, the Czech animator, paid homage to this tradition with his beautifully made puppet films of the 1950s and '60s, the best known of which was an adaptation of Shakespeare's *Midsummer Night's Dream* (see Figure 1.1).

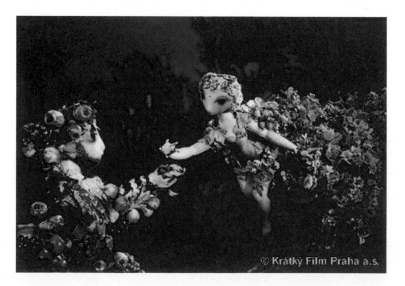

Figure 1.1 Titania and Oberon from *A Midsummer Night's Dream* by Jiri Trnka, Czechoslovakia 1958 © Kratsky Film

nature and caricature

Why don't we just copy from live reference frame by frame? Surely it would save a lot of time and worry. Rotoscoping is used in 2D and computer animation in addition to motion capture techniques to get around some problems. This is literally copying frame by frame off live film. Rotoscoping was used extensively in Disney's *Snow White*, for instance where Snow White dances around the well singing *Some Day my Prince Will Come*. It is a technique employed to speed up the animation process, similar to motion capture in computer animation. But straight copying can look strangely lifeless because animation is an art, not just a skill. What the animator is aiming for is to create something more than mere imitation, to create a performance.

Ladislaw Starewitch, one of the earliest experimenters in puppet animation, astonished audiences all over Europe with his animated insects and animals in such films as *The Cameraman's Revenge* (1911), *The Tale of the Fox* (1929–30) and *The Mascot* (1933). Starewitch remembered trying to animate a frog (Figure 1.2): 'I had a lot of trouble making him swim in such a way that seemed right. At first I did the movements exactly as they would have been with a real frog. But on screen it just didn't work, so I animated his movements almost caricaturally and it came out much better.'

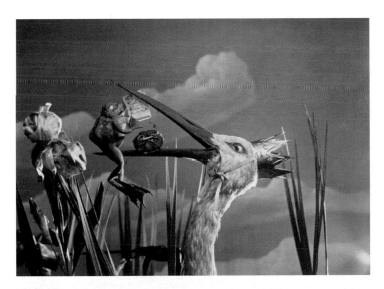

Figure 1.2 *The Frogs Who Wanted a King/Frogland/Les Grenouilles qui Demandent Un Roi* by Ladislas Starewitch 1927. © L.B. Martin-Starewitch

Sometimes caricature is intrinsic to the characters' design. Just as Trnka's puppets where the static faces have an eloquence, Nick Park's Wallace and Gromit have an economy of design that allows a range of emotions to be described with the smallest of movements. Brow up: happiness, innocence, worry, enquiry. Brow down: suspicion, frustration, anger, mild annoyance and determination.

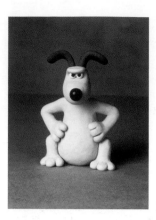

Figure 1.3 Gromit. © Aardman/W&G Ltd 1989

Extreme reactions of the 2D *Who Framed Roger Rabbit* or Tex Avery style are not normally the province of the model animator. Working with Plasticine has certain restrictions and armatures cannot be stretched to express extremes of emotion. The model animator is working in a subtler arena, where body language is employed to greater effect. This is not to say model animation precludes extremes. The use of replacements or substitutes in model animation allows plenty of 'stretch and squash'. A model is made for each different movement, so that the animator replaces a new model for each shot. When shooting on 2s this could mean you are using 12 different models per second of film. (Shooting on 2s is explained in chapter 3, page 22.) Using this method means everything has to be very well planned in advance, but it does allow you to stretch a pose as far as you want. It was originally employed by George Pal in the 1940s for films such as *Tulips will Grow* and *Home on the Range*. More recently, *Pingu,* the delightful series about a penguin created by Otmar Gutmann, was made with replacements – even props were repeated as replacements. Pingu was a great example of the wheel being reinvented.

> *I was probably more influenced by drawn cartoons: Tex Avery and Tom and Jerry stuff, rather than Trnka and George Pal. Even though you would look back on that stuff now and say 'Wow!' – I wasn't really aware of any of that as a kid. It didn't grab me as much as stretch and squash. I suppose that came from Morph (Aardman) and Disney. The performances in the drawn stuff had more life to it, rather than the wooden stuff. That's why I liked Morph so much – it felt more flexible. It had more gags. And I suppose the style comes from just wanting to give something more reality. Instead of a blob with two holes in it – you want to give it a bit more reality – or something more silly.*
> Jeff Newitt – director on *Trainspotter, Loves Me Loves Me Not,*
> animated Mr and Mrs Tweedy on *Chicken Run*

There are many interpretations of model animation, stop motion or 3D animation. Two Americans working in Britain, the brothers Quay, use found objects to imbue their lyrical and sometimes nightmarish films with atmosphere, for example in *The Street of Crocodiles* and

This Unnameable Little Broom. Their style derives from an Eastern European tradition of fairy tale and fable and has been described as 'bringing dead matter to life'.

Jan Svankmajer, another Czech filmmaker, whose more surreal animation ranges from clay animation to pixillation, has influenced many filmmakers including Dave Borthwick of bolexbrothers, who directed *The Secret Adventures of Tom Thumb* as a combination of pixillated live characters acting alongside 8″ animated puppets. Pixillation (not to be muddled with pixelation) is moving a normally live object, like a human, frame by frame to create something that moves very differently!

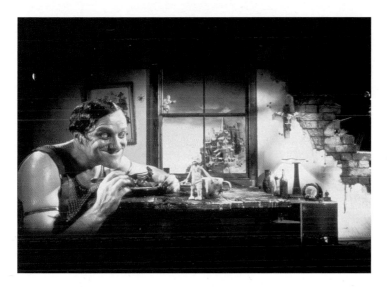

Figure 1.4 *The Secret Adventures of Tom Thumb* by bolexbrothers. © Manga Entertainment Ltd 2002

In the USA a different kind of model animation came into being with Willis O'Brien's *The Lost World,* made in 1925, and *King Kong*, made in 1933. O'Brien, and the assistant who joined him in 1948 to work on *Mighty Joe Young*, Ray Harryhausen, have probably been the greatest inspiration for today's model animators. Harryhausen's pioneering work with armatures and latex, not to mention his superb drawing and bronze casting skills, laid the ground for many of the techniques still used today. His animation had a more natur-alistic movement than seen before, and his animation of the skeletons in *Jason and the Argonauts* (1963) is one of his most enduring sequences studied by animators. Harryhausen's work has influenced most of the animators mentioned in this book, among them film-makers like Phil Tippett, who has brought his skills to bear on a whole genre of fantasy and space-legend films, like *Dragonslayer*, *Jurassic Park* and the *Star Wars* films, and who is in turn influencing the next generation of animators.

Several years ago the conversations in animation studios revolved around the advent of computer animation heralding the demise of model animation. Now we are beginning to

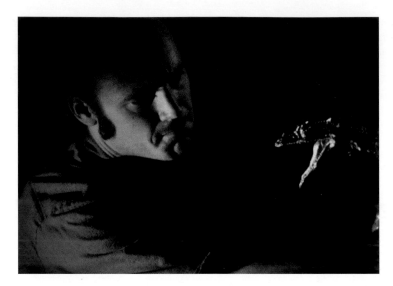

Figure 1.5 Phil Tippett animating on *Dragonslayer*. © Tippett Studio 1982

see model animation studios embrace CGI (computer-generated images), sometimes due to budgetary considerations, but more often because it gives them the freedom to use many more tools, and develop their ideas with fewer constraints. Skilled model animators are able to translate their work on to the computer screen, as 2D or 3D. As always it is creativity and imagination that harness the tools to the best effect. However many animators feel computer animation is strangling the creative process of model animation – which is based on the tension of giving a performance. As Guionne says at the start of this chapter 'all of a sudden you are that puppet and you move how that puppet moves...' This is clearly an achievement that it does not seem possible to replicate with the process of character animation on a computer. It is perhaps a harder transition for someone who has grown up with that desire to bring a 3D character to life, than a 2D animator who already works in that 'constructional' way.

what this book is for

This book is to help those who want to learn the hands-on, tactile craft skill (the artistry is up to you). These are just the basics – you can use the principles explained for whatever animation medium you work in. As computer technology develops – even now there are experiments with sensations of weight, where the operator has a tactile sense of what they are moving. It may be that the animator can drive the technology into a medium responsive enough to be suitable for model animation, so that the animator has the same tactile control over a puppet and can derive that same sense of having given a performance. Although that seems like going a long way round to achieve what we have now: hands, minds and talent.

> When it's working you feel like an artist – it's great. Getting there can be very difficult because it's so time-consuming – it's such a long period of time. It's pure faith that keeps me going. I find along the way people who want to work with me,

lighting people, musicians. There's a handful who have the same love of creation that jives with what I'm doing. Nobody's making any money – but we're making something beautiful, for the sake of it.

Tim Hittle – US animator, directed the Oscar-nominated short Canhead, and The Potato Hunter, animator on Monkeybone, Nightmare Before Christmas and James and the Giant Peach

chapter 2

getting equipped

chapter summary

- *what is your aim?*
- *recording formats*
- *film*
- *video/DV*
- *animation software/frame grabbers*
- *essential and non-essential extras*
- *the animator's toolkit*
- *lighting*
- *editing/sound*
- *rough guide to film/video or DV recording budgets*
- *glossary*

I started trying to tell stories when I was young at home, I wanted to tell stories in some shape or form, and I was into drawing cartoons. In our house, none of the relations had film gear or anything like that. So you try and get your head round it. 'I want to make a film...how's it done?' How do you make a film?

I drew onto tracing paper, mounted those drawings into slides and projected them, and made a little recording to go with it. You try to make more of the story rather than think of the production values – because there aren't any production values! You just try to do an entertaining something!

Jeff Newitt

what is your aim?

If you've got a story to tell, you will find a way. It is much easier, much cheaper now to make a film, but somehow, the choices are far more complex... Is your animation to show in your own home to your friends and relations? Are you working at college on semi-professional equipment? Are you hoping to enter your film into a festival? Have you got funding on the strength of a pilot and now need to make broadcast quality animation? Whichever it is you need to tailor the equipment you choose to your needs. Basically, to record your animation you will need a camera, a tripod and some lights. Whether you want to record onto film, video or digitally is discussed below. You may want to record sound and have some way of editing. The choices are various and the proliferation of frame capture, sound and editing software have made the animation process, if not simpler, at least far more accessible.

I have listed various options of equipment set-ups at the end of this chapter, ranging from second-hand to professional equipment. I cannot go into detail about uses and practice, I can only skim the surface – it is always worth approaching a professional in the field for advice. If you are starting from scratch, and don't know anyone with the same interests, look out for any local film and video workshops – they might not be experts in animation, but will understand the equipment.

recording formats

You will need to choose whether you are going to shoot your animation on film, video or digitally. It's a question of money, more than anything. Home video and Super 8 is the cheapest, most accessible, and quickest to get going with. At the other end of the scale there is 35mm film, used by professionals for commercials and features. Obviously the cheaper your equipment, the lower the quality of the image. This is fine for getting your work seen if you are applying to an animation course, or entering your work into some film festivals, or sending your animation show-reel around companies – what people are looking for there is the quality of your animation. It helps though, if you are looking for work, that the quality looks as good as you can manage, as competition is fierce.

The choices between film and video can be very personal, the pros and cons can be argued. Film and digital video (DV) is not always as expensive as you are led to believe, and each have their own attractions. Now that you can record and edit on your home computer it is possible to shoot on all formats and load the result into your computer for post production (editing).

When choosing your format, it is as well to consider post production: you will need to grade the colour, compensate for any set shift (your set can get bumped, or shrink and expand with temperature changes) and you may want to remove some supporting rigs that are in shot. Also consider the cost of editing; it may be that you know someone with a semi-professional edit suite using Final Cut Pro or a base level Avid that will help your production, but should be catered for in your budget. DVD is becoming a cheaper and more accessible way of presenting your work.

film

Film gauges: Super 8mm, 16mm, Super 16mm, 35mm – these refer to the width of the film: the wider the film, the more information and detail you can get onto a single frame, therefore the better quality the image. Super 16mm is a wider version of 16mm.

Nowadays once you've filmed your animation, your negative can be **telecine'd** (transferred) by the film processing labs or at a post-production house onto whatever format you want to edit it on: VHS, mini DV, DVD, Beta SP (professional video format), or Digibeta (professional digital video format). This can then be loaded onto whichever editing package you are using on a computer. If then you want the film for exhibition at cinemas, you can have it output back onto 16mm or 35mm print stock once you have edited. Many festivals also show the video format: Beta SP. If you do wish to edit your film manually on film editing equipment, you will need to tell the labs that you want a 'rush' print, a relatively cheap, un-graded print of your negative original.

When buying a second-hand film camera it should be tested for registration, light tightness, flicker and focus. This means that the film is held steady in exactly the same place in front of the **gate** each time. Check that claws aren't worn, that they are correctly tensioned, and that the drive mechanism is moving smoothly. Always run off some film as a test, both **single-frame** and at normal running speed. Try single-frame at the beginning and middle and end of a test, with some normal speed in between. Leave the film loaded in the camera in a lit room to check for light tightness.

super 8mm film

Super 8mm film is an acceptable format for relatively cheap filmmaking. Standard 8mm is used very little and is hard to find processing for, but Super 8mm is undergoing a bit of a renaissance at the moment; people seem to have a nostalgic need for the quality of film. But there are some limitations with processing that could slow up your production. One roll (50 ft) of Super 8mm runs for 2 minutes 30 seconds.

super 8mm cameras

Using second-hand Super 8mm equipment is not always going to be a reliable way of animating. Always look for one with a single-frame facility. They should take a **cable release** – this is a device that fits onto the camera that allows you to press the trigger without touching the camera, therefore reducing any camera 'jog'. The checking procedure for the mechanism mentioned before should be used. Super 8mm cameras are not being made any more.

16mm film

This is still a favourite with many animators, although finding a decent second-hand camera and lenses can be difficult, and is getting more expensive. *Bob the Builder*, a popular children's TV series, is shot on Super 16mm, a wider frame format. Super 16 is a useful format as it can be blown up to 35mm for a low budget feature and is suitable for origination on to high definition TV. 16mm comes in 100ft and 400ft rolls. The former runs for 2 minutes 40 seconds at 25 fps. Converting a Bolex to Super 16 (if you get the job done at Bolex Paillard in Switzerland) will cost about £1100.

16mm cameras

The most popular of the 16mm cameras to be used for stop frame is the Bolex. Created by the Swiss company, Bolex Paillard, Bolex cameras were originally designed as news cameras. They are compact and the clockwork (spring motor) versions have been used through most of the last century by independent film-makers and animators. All H16s have single-frame facility and a reputation for steady registration. The Bolex can be converted to Super 16mm, a format acceptable for TV production.

The Bolex H16 RX5 is probably the most popular for stop-frame animation. You will need a Bolex adapter for the trigger button, and a Bolex cable release, as you don't want to touch the camera while filming. You can use your RX camera without a single-frame unit for animation. But for a perfect result, you should use a single-frame unit – a motor which ensures absolutely constant exposure time for every frame. This prevents the slight flicker which inevitably results from using a spring motor. It fits onto the side of the camera on a 1:1 shaft (Figure 2.1).

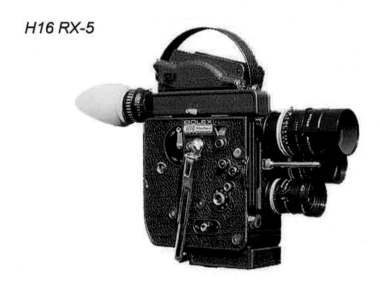

Figure 2.1 Bolex H16 RX5. Courtesy Chambless Cine Equipment

A daylight loading roll for a Bolex takes 100 ft, which represents 2 minutes 40 seconds of film. Don't be fooled by the term 'daylight'; it is best to load cameras in subdued light. You have to play safe as so much time and money is at stake with animation. Film stock information can be found on the Kodak and the Fuji websites. For that and information on processing laboratories look in appendix 1.

A good source of information in the UK about everything to do with the Bolex is Andrew Alden, who has written several books on the subject and deals in second-hand Bolex cameras. See appendix 1.

35mm film

This is not an option to be considered by the beginner, but I have included it as it is how many professional animators work. 35mm is still the favourite for commercials and feature films as it still presents the very best visual quality. 35mm film (400 ft) runs for 4 minutes 27 seconds at 25 fps.

35mm cameras

The price is prohibitive to the beginner unless you've won the lottery or come into some big money. The most commonly used camera for animation is the Mitchell, an old live action camera that has been heavily modified for use in animation since 1928, and was used on *King Kong* in 1933. It is still used for commercial work.

The major drawback with film in the past has been that it has to be processed at a film laboratory before you can see what you have shot. This caused much anguish when film returned from the labs with mistakes either in the filming or the animation. However, now you can use **video assist**, a video camera placed close to the side of your film camera outputting to a computer with frame-grabbing software (see below). This has made life much easier for the animator who can see whether a move is working or not before committing it to film.

lenses and accessories

For a 16mm camera a zoom lens is your best choice. This gives you a good range of frame sizes to work with; from 12mm, a good wide angle that will give a sense of depth to your set, to 120mm, which is probably closer than you would want to be. Prime or fixed focal length lenses start to get very expensive, with a relatively rare 10mm Switar for the Bolex going for about £500+. A set of four prime lenses: a 12mm wide angle, a 16mm, a 25mm (25mm is near to standard eyesight) and a 50mm, will give you better optical quality than the zoom lens, but is a heavy investment.

To get a closer focussed shot than you can with standard lens, you can use a **diopter**. These are supplementary lenses, useful on miniature sets, that come ranging from $\frac{1}{4}$ diopter to a +2 diopter, depending on how much magnification you need. Alternatively you can use extension tubes that fit between the camera body and the lens to focus closer.

And if you are using film, you will need a **light meter**, a device for measuring the amount of light you are exposing on to your film. This is also useful for manual video cameras, but on the whole not necessary for basic video and digital recording, as they have automatic exposure.

video/DV

domestic analogue video

The home video camera/camcorder is great for starting out, relatively cheap and simple to use. You can plug it into your computer if you have a **USB/S** video connection and are using single frame animation software. This is perfect for learning and practising on, fine for applying to courses and companies and acceptable for some festivals. You would do best to find a camera that has manual controls (exposure, focus and zoom); many video cameras have no manual over-ride, which can be infuriating when you are trying to create moody scenes and you have to end up tweaking the gain switch.

digital video

Probably the best image quality you can get for low-cost film-making. You can use a digital stills camera, but they can give you quite a variation of exposure from frame to frame, and require more storage on your hard drive as they tend to be higher resolution. A digital video camera is better designed for continuous frame storage than a stills camera, but then, as always, you have to balance the cost against your aims. It also plugs straight into your computer using either a **USB** or a **Firewire** connection.

webcam

A low-cost, low-resolution solution, using the USB connection to computer. This is a simple and very affordable way to get into stop motion and get a feel for it, doing animation tests. The quality, however, is poor for anything other than web-based projects.

animation software/frame grabbers

Up until the 1980s animators worked 'blind', not being able to see the results of their handiwork until the film came back from the labs the next day or perhaps a week later. Inevitably this caused stress and sleepless nights, but that was how it was, and many traditional animators would say it gave them an edge that's been lost now that you can check every frame. Barry Bruce, Creative Director at Vinton's, the US studio famous for Claymation©, maintains it has slowed animation up. Working blind, they say, gives you a flow and a more instinctive feel for the animation that is unique to model animators. There's no denying that, for the less than super-skilled animators, frame grabbing, or frame capture software is a godsend. It allows you to capture your animation, with a camera feeding images frame by frame, into a computer. You review your frame before 'grabbing' it and if you are satisfied with it, you can store it, and compare it to your live image. This way you can see how your animation is progressing frame by frame. You should be able to overlay your live image over your stored image, and see exactly how far to move limbs, drapery and hairs. You can go backwards and forwards frame by frame, or set up a loop, to show the animation in real time up to your current 'live' image.

In the late 80s in the UK, animators were using tape-based video assist systems with single-frame facility. The PVR (Perception Video Recorder) made by the Canadian company Digital Processing Systems, was a device for computer graphic artists to render onto and play back their animation in real time without the need for an expensive tape-based system. Cosgrove Hall and Aardman Animations had both waited many years for animator-friendly software. David Sproxton, director of Aardman Animations, remembers:

> We saw it at the Cardiff Animation Festival, around 1990/1. As it recorded video on a frame-by-frame basis it seemed ideal for our needs. We had extensive faxes going back and forth to Canada describing our needs. Eventually they sent a guy over to talk to us and things started to happen. The 'Animate' system was really the culmination of our requests and others over the course of several years.

The PVR developed by DPS and the equivalent DAR (Digital Animation Recorder) made by EOS are used in many companies and colleges around the world and have helped to make the model animation process more accessible. They are excellent tools, and can produce broadcast quality animation, but of course they are expensive. The updated system from DPS, 'Reality', PVR's replacement, still using the **Animate** software retails at around £5000–£6000 for the whole package, including the computer, monitors etc., and the EOSdv7 (replacing the DAR) retails at a little less.

However, as one would expect, coming on the market all the time are less expensive, very useful animation software packages that can essentially cover similar functions to the PVR. One of the most versatile of these is **Stop Motion Pro** and **Stop Motion Lite**, an Australian product that is fast gaining a foothold in the educational community. The software on its own costs under £200. However, at present, Stop Motion Pro is only PC compatible. There other similar packages like **BTV Pro** and **Framethief** that are compatible with Apple Macs. You will want a large amount of memory and storage on the computer: a minimum of 96 MB RAM with a 360 × 288 capture card, although Stop Motion Pro works better on the recommended spec of 720 × 576 capture card and 128 MB RAM.

In the more accessible bracket, Stop Motion Pro is nearer in its facilities to the Animate system than packages like Adobe Premiere. It allows total control of every frame, flipping between the previously shot frame and the 'live' frame (waiting to be shot). It also enables superimposing or onion-skinning both the previous and the live frame and the ability to delete frames if necessary. Onion-skinning is a term used for being able to see one frame superimposed on another – thus being able to see the degree of movement you have created between the recorded and the live frame.

Your computer should ideally have a **USB** or **Firewire** interface. If you have both you can support analogue video and digital inputs. Some animation frame capture software will work only with DV camcorders with Firewire connection, and others will work only with analogue camcorders (USB or **S video** connections). You will also need a compatible video capture card. Some animation video capture software may allow you to go through the USB connection and may not require a video capture card (again, it depends on frame capture software). Video capture cards can cost from £200, but sometimes have the benefit of being sold along with a software package, so it depends on your dealer and some informed negotiation.

To get right away from the nightmare of which animation software or video capture card to choose there is the extremely straight-forward **Lunchbox**. This is the simplest set-up of all and is a great learning tool. Simply plug your video camera and monitor into this stand-alone animation system. It is a hardware device used to create and test animation, without the aid of a computer. It is digital, in that all the video is digitized. However, it only has analogue input and output. Many animators are finding this a very friendly way to work.

The LunchBox Sync model 3000P (PAL) model for European use can store at least $6\frac{1}{2}$ minutes of animation, although you can get an extra storage facility that allows you to store 18 times that amount. There is an NTSC version for use in the USA.

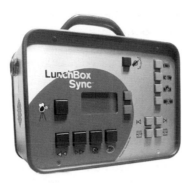

Figure 2.2 LunchBox Sync. Courtesy Howard Mozeico © Animation Toolworks

essential and non-essential extras

Something solid on which to put your camera: a **tripod**. And no matter on which format you shoot, your tripod has got to be solid. It can of course have its feet glued into place with the glue gun, but if the legs are flimsy it'll let you down. You need a tripod with at the very least a head that you can pan and tilt, and that locks off firmly. If you are shooting with a 16mm film camera, you will want a more solid tripod than one designed for a domestic camcorder. Most domestic video tripods come with their **heads** attached. But if you were to find an old wooden tripod there are a variety of different heads for different sensitivities of movement. The **friction head**, the simplest form of pan and tilt movement, is designed for live filming and cannot be reliably used for controlled camera moves. It's perfect for 'locked-off' shots. The **fluid head** is also used for 'live' filming as it has a cushioned, smooth movement that is not particularly helpful for animation. The **geared head** is far more expensive, but gives you a *controllable*, smooth movement. This suggests that trying to create camera moves using the ordinary heads is not going to be easy, which is why the professionals use immense computer-controlled robot arms for **motion control**. Because it is preferable, when making your first films, to concentrate on the animation rather than trying to create flashy camera moves, a locked-off friction head is the best bet.

If you have to do a camera move, a Manfrotto geared head (second-hand approx. £150), on a sturdy tripod, gives you more control over your camera movements. There are far bigger, heavier heads which would only be used professionally: the Worral head, Moy head, etc. Nowadays the heads will be motorized for motion control, but it is possible to do your moves by hand, with a taped pointer on the head, and marked tape on the track.

A **tracker bed** that can take the geared head will enable smoother tracking. However this kind of specialized equipment is hard to find second hand, and will be expensive. But an animation studio that has updated to more sophisticated motion control may be able to lend one.

the animator's toolkit

Apart from modelling tools, which are always a personal choice, you will need a comprehensive toolkit including **G-clamps**, to hold your world together, every kind of pliers, screwdrivers, but probably the most useful piece of equipment for the animator is a **stop-watch**. Timing, the basis of all animation, takes practice. Imagine or observe the move, practice the move yourself, timing your speed; break the move down into actions and then time those actions. The more you do it the less you will need to rely on a stopwatch.

You will also need a **mirror** as you need to understand movement: look at yourself, study how you move, look at your expressions. Always have a small mirror on your set – or a large mirror somewhere that you can study yourself in.

Another useful piece of kit is a **hot glue gun**. It's a reliable and handy way of fixing things down. It is important that nothing moves in each shot, or the story's credibility is blown. The glue gun shouldn't be used on a good floor or table surface for obvious reasons. Alternatively there is always **'gaffer' tape** or **duct tape**, for use instead of a glue gun; it's tough and very sticky, useful for taping down cables that clutter the floor. It has a hundred other uses.

Whether or not you have a frame-grabbing (see below) device that allows you to flip between your live and your stored image, you might want to use a **gauge**, a device to keep track of how far you are moving your model. It can be a sophisticated engineer's surface gauge, or can be home made, using any method that will give you a flexible and precise pointer to keep a clear track of your movements.

Keep **wet wipes** at hand to keep your hands clean. They should be lanolin-free and as non-fibrous as possible – the best type in the UK are Boots own brand. They are also wonderful for cleaning pen marks off a monitor.

lighting

Available light (as opposed to created light) is not an option with animation – daylight will change dramatically while you are filming and affect your image greatly. So you need to create an artificially lit set.

The simplest form of low-cost lighting would be with two articulated desk, or anglepoise lamps, so long as they can be locked off tightly and don't 'drift' during your shot. If the light is too low you will reduce your depth of field (the area of your set that is in focus) which may present problems.

Another low-cost form of lighting to try out is fluorescent light tubes, you can get daylight or tungsten balanced tubes that'll give you a good overall light as well as keeping your set cooler than with conventional lighting.(very important). Fluorescent lighting can give your film a green cast, but colour correction filters are available for this.

A wide range of lighting is available from film and theatre lighting distributors. Ask if there's any ex-demonstration lighting, sometimes they sell on ex-hire stock. Hiring lighting is a possibility, but in hiring any equipment for animation, the length of the shoot is a strong consideration.

Filming on a normal domestic electric circuit you can't use more than 3100 watts, which means you can use one 2K lamp with a selection of smaller ones if you need to light a large set. Theatrical or film lighting has more controllability in that you can focus the beam, and they also have attachments making it easier to add filters or diffusers.

But for accessible, low-cost lighting, photofloods and mini spots are available from photographic shops. Halogen lamps in the range of 150–300 W (known as 'garage' lamps) are available from most DIY stores and are useful for a wide throw of light. For lighting smaller areas or a smaller set, mini reflector 12 V 50 W halogen lights can be used with a transformer and a dimmer, again available from DIY stores. You can also get 6 V 30 W spots that can throw a narrow beam, useful for back lighting, or rim lighting (see chapter 11 – filming). For little practical lights to use on the set, you can use torch bulbs and Christmas tree bulbs.

editing/sound

A number of editing and sound packages are available. Final Cut Pro (Mac) is a semi-professional editing package becoming very popular, and, considering it is relatively cheap, it is being used more and more by professionals, as editors find they can work from their home computers. A sophisticated post-production package is After Effects made by Adobe, and a popular and well-used product is Adobe Premiere. But there is a large choice of editing software available and it's a question of choosing what you're happiest with, within your budget.

As for film editing, it's possible to pick up second-hand Super 8mm and 16mm editing equipment: a manual pic sync (picture synchronizer – for synching magnetic sound track to picture); a film splicer (a mini guillotine for manually cutting film and soundtrack); a film bin (allowing the film to reel off the pic sync into a, hopefully, dust free cotton sack while you roll the film back and forth, thus protecting the film from scratching); and a Steenbeck (for viewing and cutting purposes). The Steenbeck is a very large and heavy piece of equipment and really only suitable for those with ample room, a garage or the like. Many colleges and companies have got rid of this equipment as it takes up much needed space – and has been superseded by digital equipment. Film is generally processed at the labs but edited digitally and matched up at the very end of the process.

recording sound

Whatever you record on, as with a camera lens, the important part is the microphone as that sources the material. You can get a decent dynamic microphone for as little as £10. Top-of-the-range would be a Neumann U87 at around £1900. Record your sound onto a Minidisc or DAT recorder. For information and advice on sound recording a good website is **www.shure.com**.

Dialogue needs to be recorded before animation if it is to be synched up with mouth movements, as you will work out your timings to your dialogue track (see chapter 8 – sound advice). To do this you can input your recording to your computer using sound editing software such as (professional) Pro-Tools or (designed specifically for animators) Magpie from Third Wish. You can then see your soundtrack displayed in a wave from – a visual translation of the sound allowing you to identify every accent down to a quarter frame. Magpie allows you to break your dialogue down into phonetic sounds so that you can work out your mouth shapes. It has its own bank of mouth shapes as a guide.

Other than dialogue, the music, atmosphere and sound effects can be created and added in the edit. You can get sound effects, atmospheres and music from library discs, but again, it is going to be a more individual project if you create the sound track as much as possible yourself.

rough guide to film/video or DV recording budgets

These are only an approximate guide, they should be checked before any purchase. You would probably do best to look further on suggested websites listed in appendix 1. I have not included editing and post-production in these costs. I have based these prices on UK research and would not recommend doing a straight conversion to US dollars or Euros as it would be wiser to check second-hand prices in your own countries. See appendix 1 for outlets.

under £300 (second-hand 8mm equipment)

8mm and Super 8mm film can be transferred to a format suitable for festival screening and can be acceptable for broadcast. These costs only go as far as processing your film.

Lights: 2 × 150W halogen lamps (available from DIY stores)	from £5
Light stands × 2	from £20
Super 8mm camera (must have single-frame facility)	from £150
Light meter	from £40
Tripod	from £40
Film: colour negative with processing	from £25
Transfer to VHS/Mini DV available per half hour min.	from £9
	(prices quoted from Pro8mm, UK)

under £1000 (second-hand 16mm equipment)

Lighting: selection of lamps from 50–500 W	from £150
Bolex H16 RX5	from £450
Single frame motor	from £200
Tripod	from £40
100ft 16mm colour neg	£25
Lab process (per 100 ft, minimum charge)	£50
Telecine to Beta (per 100 ft, minimum charge)	£65
	(prices quoted by Technicolor Laboratories UK)

under £2000

DV camcorder/video camera	from £250
Tripod	from £40
Computer (as above)	from £500

Computer monitor	from £200
Video capture card	from £200
Animation software (Stop Motion Pro, BTV Pro, Framethief)	from £50
14" video monitor	from £200
Lighting: selection of lamps from 50–1000 W	from £350

under £3500

Lunch Box Sync 3000P (PAL)	£2335
Shipping	£86
MultiReel (optional)	£334
DV camcorder	from £450
Tripod	from £40
14" video monitor	from £200
Lighting: selection of lamps from 50–1000 W	from £350

glossary

firewire: a very fast external bus computer connection. A single port can be used to connect up 63 external devices.

gaffer tape: wide, tough and very sticky fabric-backed tape available from electrical suppliers also known as duct tape.

gate: opening on a camera behind the lens where the film is exposed, frame by frame.

dope sheet/X-sheets or bar charts: dope sheets and bar charts are marked up paper pads used in the planning of animation. The dope sheet helps plan the specific timings of action, dialogue, music, sound effects and camera instructions. They are used in conjunction with the storyboard to map out and plan animation sequences in terms of story-telling, film-making, cinematography and narrative. Bar charts are more specifically just for dialogue. In the US and in computer animation these are called X-sheets, or exposure sheets.

registration: as the film is passing through the camera it stops in front of the gate, is held steady (in registration) while being exposed and is then pulled down. If the film moves in the gate at all, the image will jump about so much, or be blurred, rendering the film impossible to watch.

single-frame: film is exposed at normal running speeds of between 18 frames (8mm) and 24 frames (16 and 35mm) per second. Video records at 25 fps (US 30 fps). Single frame means exposing one frame of film at a time. Video actually records two 'fields' for every frame.

S-Video: S VHS: Super VHS connector.

telecine: film labs' term for transferring film to video or digital format.

U-Matic: an old tape-based video system.

USB (universal serial bus): an external computer connection for mice, keyboards etc.

chapter 3

getting animated

I began making films as a teen on my own in the late seventies. I never attended any kind of film school. I worked in Super 8 and managed over the years to make a series of short, rough and cheap films. Learning to pull off good animation was my main motivation. I soon came to realise that it was important to make a complete film, not just a string of pointless animation tests that no one would want to watch. Then the clay characters became actors telling a story and it all was much more interesting.

Tim Hittle

animating familiar objects as a first approach

Your aim is to make a story in which your characters are the actors. If you start from the very beginning thinking about giving a performance, even the exercises suggested in this chapter will become imbued with life. It is the key to character animation, and will take the dryness out of any practice work that you do. The exercises included all have a practical basis, but in order to keep them interesting, think about giving the piece of Plasticine, or matchbox that little bit of character that will bring it to life.

This chapter doesn't give those character animation tips, you will progress on to that later. My suggestion is that if you begin by thinking of exercises in terms of performance, you will get there quicker.

First of all, before you attempt something more elaborate, pick some everyday objects and try to breathe a little life into them. Don't give yourself extra work such as rigging to stop something falling over, or having to articulate 'limbs' that flop around and need stiffening, or over-complicate things by building sets and constructing armatures. Take some time to play around and experiment with the materials you might work with. Inanimate objects are a good way of learning about animation and character. If you just take a matchbox and try to imagine it as a dog or a car and then start giving it dog/car characteristics. For instance, the dog wants you to throw a ball for it. So it's panting, wagging its tail and jumping up and down. It quickly becomes apparent that it's quite hard to do this or to make your matchbox look like anything at all, let alone a panting terrier. And yet, while you're practising – and this doesn't have to be filmed at this stage – what you are doing is imagining all the movements this dog is making, you are thinking about the timing of the movements and you are taking the first crucial steps in the process.

If you can start to get some recognizable 'doggy' movements out of this matchbox you'll have some understanding of the *performance* of animation, then think how much easier it will be when you are using a toy dog, or even an articulated puppet dog!

timing: single frame or double frame?

The first principle of animation is based on persistence of vision: the way your eye joins up consecutive still images to make a moving image, and the amount of difference from one image to the next that the eye will tolerate and translate as a fluid movement. Film and video is projected at 24 (film) 25 (TV) frames per second. These speeds were arrived at as being an optimum number of images per second for the eye to perceive smooth movement. In the UK, Europe and Australia, wherever mains frequency is 50 Hz, video playback is at 25 frames per second. In the States and Japan, where video plays back at 30 frames per second, it is based on a mains frequency of 60 Hz. The playback speed for computers is variable: digital formats such as Mpeg, the highest quality digital files, will play at 30 fps but Quicktime will play from 10–15 fps, Quicktime 3 at 15 fps, and RealMedia plays at 3–6 fps. This would require a different approach, and generally, in this book I am basing the animation on 24/25 frames per second.

However this does not necessarily mean that in animation you have to produce 24 or 25 *different* movements per second in order to create an acceptable flow of movement. You learn to calculate whether you can convey convincing movement by changing the move every two frames, more or less.

Should you work in singles or double frames? Ones or twos? It depends on the movement. Single frame is when you move on every frame, so there are 24/25 different shots per second. This creates a very fluid, smooth movement, useful for hand gestures or a flag waving. If you are shooting a very fast action it might require shooting on ones. Shooting on twos is quite acceptable and in fact the animators at Aardman tend to favour twos to keep a lively sense of action. Nick Park prefers working fast and not getting bogged down by too much technique: 'I don't notice technical smoothness – that doesn't interest me – that can work against a character sometimes.' However that would not stop him using single framing in certain situations. For instance if you are filming someone running across the screen in six frames, very fast, you will need to shoot on singles, or the movement won't even register with the viewer.

Use a stopwatch to help get used to timing. Get used to counting seconds, half seconds and so on, tapping out the rhythms, so that when you make a hand gesture, or bounce a ball off the floor, count out the move.

Anthony Scott, who animated Jack in *Nightmare Before Christmas* suggests:

> *Say 'one-thousand-one' as you're acting out your motion. Then use this to figure out frame count:*
>
> *one = 6 frames*
> *one-thou = 12 frames*
> *one-thousand = 18 frames*
> *one-thousand-one = 24 frames. I use it all the time, it's a built-in stopwatch.*

When you start to study a movement for timing, you first of all break it down into seconds, then you break it down into frames.

As you get to understand animation, you learn that to hold for longer can convey certain movements or emotions, or if you are filming a fast action, it may be you need to shoot it one frame per move.

notes on movement

The bouncing ball is always given as a starting point in animation training because it is a simple way of looking at movement and the forces that make things move. It brings together many of the principles of animation in one simple exercise and is all based on physics: Newton's three laws of motion, which if you really want to know, are that:

- An object at rest remains at rest until acted upon by a force; an object in motion continues moving in a straight line at constant velocity until acted upon by a force.
- Acceleration of an object is directly proportional to the force acting on the object and inversely proportional to its mass.
- For every action there is an equal and opposite reaction.

It's not necessary to understand these laws in depth, but when you start looking at things falling, or balls bouncing and hitting walls, or a car skidding around a corner, you start thinking about gravity and friction acting upon things and then you are beginning to understand movement.

As an animator you need to:

1. give weight to inanimate objects: you need to consider how long it will take for a rock or a leaf to fall.
2. give weight and movement to a living creature. You want the audience to believe your puppet is a living, breathing, thinking entity in its own right, so it should have a 'life force' of its own.

By getting right back to the basics of movement, you can learn how to give weight, thought and vitality to your puppets.

If a ball is thrown into the air, the force throwing it is the person, the force causing it to slow and drop to the ground is gravity. The heavier the object, the more force is needed to move it, so when animating a heavy object, start it off slower than you would a light object.

A movement builds up speed and then slows down again to a stop, unless it is interrupted. If you lift your hand, the movement will start slowly, then slow down again before stopping.

If you roll a ball along the ground, unless it bumps into something, it will eventually slow down and stop. The force that puts it into motion is you, the force that slows it down is gravity, and friction (the surface of the ground).

A sense of weight is created by how much time you give a movement: very simply, a creature that moves slowly seems heavier, a dinosaur, an elephant, or a giant lumbers slowly along. A creature that moves quickly seems lighter, a scurrying mouse or a scuttling insect. The quicker a creature can gather speed, the lighter or younger it is; the slower, the heavier or older. For example: a heavy person will take longer to get up from a chair than a light person, but not necessarily be slower to sit down again, as gravity is helping them.

To give your object a slow start, you would give it a very small movement each frame, gradually increasing the amount you move it until you come up to speed, then again decreasing the movements until you stop. This is known as easing or cushioning in and out.

If you were to animate a ball being dropped to the ground, the movements would be close together for the first few frames and then, on each successive frame, the movements would get wider apart because the ball is accelerating at 9.8 metres per second per second. As the ball is not going to slow up before hitting the ground, there would be no decrease in increments.

There are situations, as in Disney's *Fantasia*, where a hippo floats on a fountain of bubbles or an elephant gets trapped inside a floating bubble. You may not want things to move realistically, but understanding the rules gives your animation credibility and, having demonstrated that you understand them, you'll get a bigger audience reaction when you break them.

first experiments: the bouncing ball

A useful exercise when starting out is the bouncing ball, useful because you learn a variety of basic skills in a relatively simple exercise. You are learning first about timing, and, second, about using timing to create an illusion of weight. You can do this under a rostrum camera, on a flat table top, or on a 45° surface if you can't get your camera right over a table. Make a 45° wooden frame to hold a flat, smooth surface for your animation. You could use a plain coloured laminated kitchen top or a piece of glass set into a frame. Make sure the camera is looking at 90° to the surface. For the ball you could use either a coin held in place with sticky wax (available at model shops) or a flat Plasticine disc that you can shape to make it squash and stretch. Make some spares.

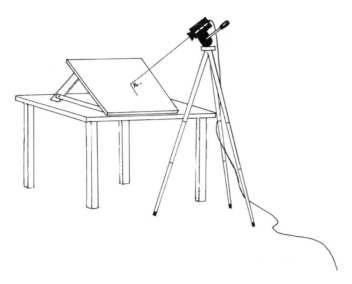

Figure 3.1 Animation exercise set-up.

Mark out where you think the ball will hit the ground first and in the following bounces. The bounces will get smaller and closer together as the ball loses energy.

The shape the ball makes in the air is a smooth parabolic curve. The ball slows down at the top of the arc, so the moves will be closer at the top. You can plan this shape on your background and give the ball a trajectory to follow, marking the increases and decreases in the speed of its movement.

The accent is at the points where the ball hits the ground, the spacing of the ball as it moves through the air will give the smooth, naturalistic movement (Figure 3.2).

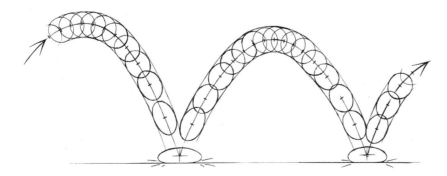

Figure 3.2 Bouncing ball parabola with exaggerated squash and stretch.
Illustration by Tony Guy

If you were to exaggerate the shape of the ball by flattening it as it hits the surface, and elongating it as it comes away from the surface, every ball will look as though it's made of soft putty. Experiment with different amounts of stretch and squash. You could give it a sense of speed by elongating it on the fall, or after the bounce of the arc. Or you can create more impact when the ball hits the ground, as if it's been thrown down, by elongating the ball at the frame before contact with the ground. Don't rely on squash and stretch as an effect you can use through all animation – it is useful to illustrate a point at this stage – to give a sense of weight there are other ways we will come to.

Try out a variety of balls. Knowing that a ball will bounce in relationship to the force applied to it and the surface it is hitting, here are some examples of the type of bounce you would expect when different forces apply. Draw your arc onto your surface as a guide, and mark off the 'increments' or measurements. Play back what you've shot and study it for timing (Figure 3.3).

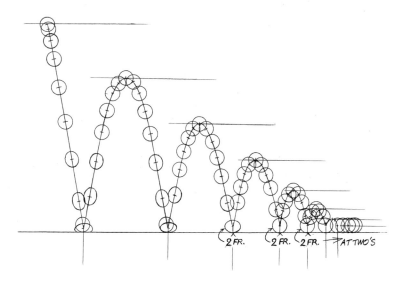

Figure 3.3 Dropping a ping pong ball. Illustration by Tony Guy

A ping pong ball is light and therefore has very little resistance, and, when dropped, can go on bouncing for some time. It is rigid and would have no squash and stretch. It will come out of a bounce very quickly. Shoot this on singles, try it with two frames on the ground so that the contact will register. Use a cut-out or a coin for this exercise.

A football would be heavier, therefore have more resistance. If it is just dropped it will not bounce as high as a ping pong ball or a tennis ball. A football is designed to be kicked. If a foot kicks a football, the foot will slow up momentarily on contact as the force is transferred to the football – the football will squash a little in taking the force of the kick and then be flung into a parabola.

A really heavy object will take more force to start it moving. To lift a cannon ball into the air takes a powerful ignition, then once it is airborne, the momentum of that force is lost against the constant force of gravity, and the cannon ball falls to earth. It will have a little bounce, rather like a bowling ball. Figure 3.4 illustrates the effect that the force has on the cannon as well (it's not necessary to create a cannon for the experiment).

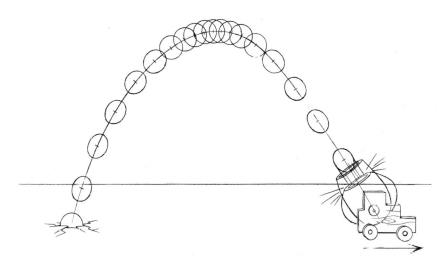

Figure 3.4 Cannon firing ball. Illustration by Tony Guy

You can extend this experiment to play with easing in and out. For instance, using the coin, just move it straight across your screen in one second (24 frames), first of all, evenly spaced. Then try easing it in at the beginning of the move, and slowing it down again at the end of the move. By trying different speeds of cushioning in and out and see what different effects this has on the action.

Using the Plasticine, make a square shape. Then animate that in the same way as the bouncing ball. Drop it in from the top of frame and decide how it's going to bounce when it hits the floor.

air resistance

A balloon has very little resistance and is susceptible to a small force: the flick of a finger or a puff of wind. Air resistance will keep the balloon up in the air. Falling leaves are slowed up on their descent to earth by air resistance, but the fine edge of the leaf will cut into that resistance, causing an erratic zig-zag descent (Figure 3.5, page 28).

the dope sheet/X-sheet

Breaking down a movement is the first stage in planning. You can use a dope sheet or X–sheet (see Figure 3.6, page 29) to express your movement in a very visual way. These are designed for 2D animators, but are used by 3D animators to chart timings, actions and

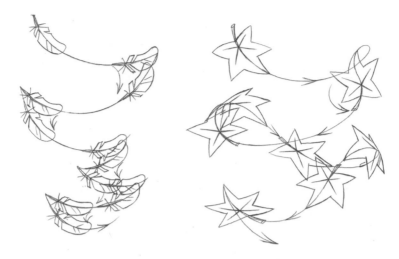

Figure 3.5 Falling leaf or feather – use the line of the leaf stem, or the feather quill, to plan your line of descent. Illustration by Tony Guy

camera moves. The sheet is divided up so that you can break your movement and dialogue down to 25 frames per second, as well as adding in any camera instructions you need.

They are available from animation suppliers (see appendix 1). Apart from helping you, this is a great way to communicate if other people are going to be helping you to animate.

planning

> To be really emphatic about the animation, it's hard to describe: but if a fist is slamming into something – like a table – you **don't** want to slow down. As the fist gets nearer to the point of contact, the increments get bigger and bigger until it slams into the table. Plan ahead well so that you're not left with a small increment when you hit the table. Plasticine is perfect for this. You can sculpt it and press it right into the table so that absolutely no light shows through, whereas a latex fist will leave a little space, a little light – it's almost impossible to get it truly flat.
>
> Pete Lord, Aardman Animations – director *Adam, War Story, The Adventures of Morph, Chicken Run*

If you were doing 2D animation you would probably plan every movement and divide it up into 'key' positions, and then plan all the in-between drawings. For obvious reasons model animators don't work this way. You start at the beginning and carry on going until you've finished. But you can work out where you need to be on your set.

UK animation director Barry Purves had a good exercise with matchboxes when he was teaching trainees at Cosgrove Hall Films in Manchester. The matchboxes were bumper cars.

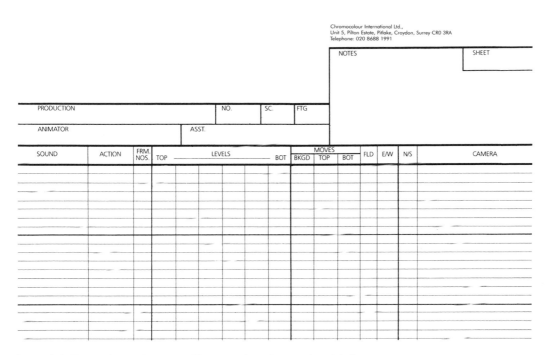

Figure 3.6 Dope sheet. Courtesy Chromacolour International Ltd

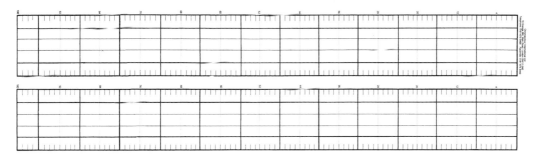

Figure 3.7 Bar chart used for sound breakdown (see chapter 8). Courtesy Chromacolour International Ltd

Two bumper cars are destined to collide. So the animator has to make sure that the movement is planned so that the collision happens at the right speed. If this shot wasn't planned, the cars could end up chasing each other round in circles, and just missing – a frustrating experience!

exercise

This is a good basic exercise in timing and planning:

1. Both cars start at the same time from standstill from different parts of the set. They need to build up speed then the speed will level out.
2. Decide what direction they are travelling, and what their route will be. You can make little invisible marks on your tabletop, marking each movement out, or put the marks on paper that you can lay down between each frame.
3. One car could take a wiggly route, the other could move in a smooth arc, but they both need to collide in say, 5 seconds.
4. Work out where the cars are going to bump into each other.
5. There is no slowing down of the speed before they collide, so there is quite an impact. This causes both cars to react by bouncing back (action and reaction). So the increments (measurements) should look as shown in Figure 3.8.

As the car builds up speed, the increments start small and increase, and similarly the increments would become smaller and smaller as the car slows down to a stop, except in this case there is no slowing down: it has collided with another object.

the old ones are the best

Try these exercises: the bouncing ball; matchbox/dodgem cars. All these exercises have been tried before by animators, and the smart ones will refer back to them over the years. They will be well-received on a showreel, because they show you have wrestled with some of the crucial principles of animation. But also try to think of better ones, and create some of your own, no more than 10 seconds long. And a word of warning – it's easy to get caught up with exercises, especially now that equipment is so much cheaper and it costs nothing other than your precious time to go over and over your animation to improve it. These exercises are valuable but don't let them inhibit you in your progress as an animator. It's quite a good idea to do an exercise once, then again to correct it – but then move straight on to another using what you've learned. Otherwise you can get bogged down in detail, which can get frustrating and hold you back. Animation is a slow process – you need to let your instincts help you where you can and not get caught up too much in the mechanics.

I always admired Pete Lord's work – with Morph and the early stuff with Vision On (BBC children's programme initially for deaf children, contained Aardman's seminal character 'Morph'). I loved the ideas – the little sketches, Plasticine characters. They would only last about a minute. There'd be somebody hoovering

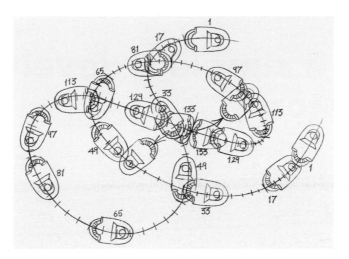

Figure 3.8 Increments on the route seen as a plan. Illustration by Tony Guy

(vacuuming) up and they would hoover up everything in the room. They would eventually hoover up themselves. Just starting in one place and seeing where they ended up – without a script. I think I like animation where you are still aware of the medium it's made in.

Nick Park

chapter 4

keep it simple – developing your story

chapter summary

- *idea – script – treatment*
- *planning your shots – basic film grammar/ composition of shots*
- *the storyboard*
- *editing – animatics and story reels*

It's normal for people to want to make something elaborate. I'd say – keep it really simple. Work within the resources you have and keep things as simple and intimate as possible – concentrate on giving a performance. Begin by giving an inanimate object some character. Even if it's only a 10 second piece that expresses a simple idea it's going to mean so much more than if you say: 'I've got this amazing storyboard' or 'I started making this model but . . .' – where's the film?

Jeff Newitt

idea – script – treatment

It's very easy to keep it simple when you have a really good idea. Sometimes the idea is great, but you can't think of the best way of expressing it. There are many different planning stages you can go through to give an idea a really good working over – then you will know after a while whether it's the business. If you are trying to sell your idea, you will need to go through quite a few drafts before presenting it to a commissioning editor. Always try to go with your instincts.

The first stage in developing your **idea** is to write a **script** and from then work out a **treatment**, where you need to start planning the look of the film, the design of the characters and just as importantly, the sound for your film. Animation is a very different process from live film-making, the main differences being that the sound is recorded first and that most of the editing is done in the planning stages. Each stage you go through helps you to

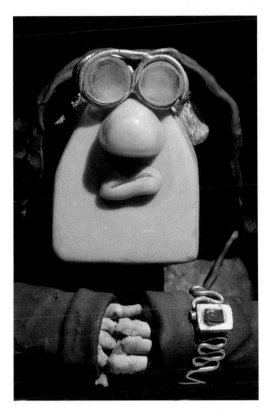

Figure 4.1 *Trainspotter* directed by Jeff Newitt and Neville Astley. Courtesy Hellzapoppin' Pictures Ltd

visualize more precisely how it is going to work. I recommend that you do go through each of these planning stages with your idea. It can seem painfully slow – but it is always worth it.

No amount of set dressing and character design will make up for a weak plot. Unless you are very happy with your script, it's not worth going to the trouble of building elaborate sets or the expense of model making. But if you have an idea really worth developing, then you need to plan properly.

the script

This is a cue for another book – scriptwriting is a craft in its own right. The main thing to remember is that you must *entertain*. And that doesn't mean you have to be funny. Entertaining people is making sure that they have really engaged with your idea – and they get some emotion from it. If your ideas are too obscure you will diminish your audience. This is not to say that you should create a film purely to please people, but if your idea has clarity and focus, it can be weird, but still entertaining. One of the clues that you're on to a good thing, apart from the obvious laughter or tears, is when people feel the hairs go up on the back of their necks. Then you know you've got them. However, you need to sustain that interest from beginning to end of your production, and that is where an experienced editor can help you.

There are many film styles your idea may fit into, or you may be creating something different. Film styles have always developed and changed and some of the early techniques for narrative film have been challenged by film-makers such as Buñuel, Hitchcock and Tarantino. Narrative film-making has also been influenced by documentaries and commercials and probably most dramatically recently, by the music video – which veers away from narrative style to a more sensory style.

find a good editor

Running your ideas past an editor at the planning stage (someone with experience of editing dramas and documentaries) will help you. Editors are skilled in knowing what works and what doesn't, filmically. You probably know something of this yourself if you go and see a lot of movies (as you should do if you are planning to make one). When you come out of the cinema, ask yourself if you liked the film: if you did, why did you like it? What made it good – what made it bad? Were you gripped from the first scene? Did your attention wander? It may have been a great idea but somehow the tension got lost and you started to think about work or food or sex . . . Editing can make or break a film. The editor is usually someone other than the director. If the director is editing their own film, it's easy for them to get carried away by their own ideas, and not always be aware of the impact they will have on an audience. So show your script to an editor, and then later, when you have a storyboard, have that properly edited too. They tend to specialize in different types of work: documentary, feature, commercial, so someone with experience of cutting short films would be the best bet.

Give your characters a history. This will help your animation later, and help them develop as real characters for your audience. Giving them a history also helps in the writing. Nick Park commented on writing Wallace and Gromit scripts:

> Now that they exist, it's much easier to write them, not just for me but because we feel like we all know them, so we know what they would do and wouldn't do. If you put them into any situation, they sort of start to write their own story, because of how they would react to that situation. It takes a little finding out. But that's what I find is a good way to write the story, to ask 'What do the characters want?' at any part in the story. Once you know what they want, you know what they will do. Otherwise you have them doing things that are just off the wall, not really motivated.

> It takes a little working out – you've got to have a good idea to start with. Just recently, I've been trying to think up new ideas for future Wallace and Gromit films – you can think of new characters that might come in, but these are more superficial, less important elements. What works is to think on the level of 'What's their dilemma? What's their problem?' rather than think what new character you could bring in. There's nothing worse than thinking 'Oh – you could have an anteater in the next one. Hmm what story could an anteater get up to?' That's difficult because that's starting with a blank piece of paper. It's better to think,

'What problem do they have where an anteater could intervene? Or mess things up! What's their issue? How does the anteater make it more complex? How does an anteater invade that situation?'

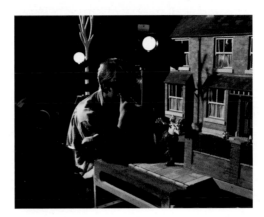

Figure 4.2 Nick Park. © Aardman/W&G Ltd 1993

treatment

The treatment puts your script into a visual format, so that you are describing what is happening as each scene unfolds: 'Fade up on a dingy rooftop, view of distant cityscape, grey, overcast sky and the sound of distant traffic. Three pigeons peck about and preen on the roof ledge. Sound of old voice croaking a song off camera. Old lady enters camera right, shuffling along, carrying washing basket . . .' This is real mental exercise and helps to order your thoughts.

planning your shots – basic film grammar/composition of shots

visualize

When you have a script you need to really start putting your characters in context. In order to storyboard your film – you have to first make some visualizations: drawings of what the scenes will look like; the world your characters inhabit. Not only do you need to make your characters believable to an audience, you need to make their world credible. This is not as difficult as it sounds, it is simply a matter of planning each stage and thinking it through – always with your audience in mind.

plan

A bit more detailed – a plan drawing (as seen from above): where are they, where are they moving to? Plot out all the character moves on a plan. Then you can start marking camera angles. Imagine yourself as the camera. What are you seeing? What do you want to see/ need to see? This can develop into a 3D cardboard mock-up, which will develop later into your set. The more you can work through in the planning stage, the better your story will become. You will sift out unnecessary information, and keep the ideas that make the story flow.

In order for your story to work, you need a sense of how your images will relate to each other to tell the story, and how the audience will see them on screen. This is called 'film grammar'. When first starting out with a script it's easy to get absorbed in detail and not look at the bigger picture. Watching other films will start to give you a feel for film grammar. The action should flow from one shot to the next, if the action suddenly changes direction, without any visual clues, the audience can be momentarily disoriented, long enough to break their concentration.

> *Watching other people's work has inspired me along the way. Bob Godfrey's Roobarb and Custard was a big influence on me. That disregard for technical slickness. It's all about execution of ideas and humour and freshness and making that whole approach attractive in itself – the wobbly lines – and in fact he even used his own voice – a very handmade approach, getting close to the medium.*
>
> Nick Park

how to angle your shots and give them continuity

First of all it is important to establish what is going on for the viewer. The **establishing shot** is generally a wide shot giving a geographical location, such as a wide shot of a room or a landscape. The viewer then can be taken in to the action. Without the establishing shot, the viewer doesn't know where they are. The director knows, because it's in their head all the time. That is what you, as director, need to remember at all times: how is the audience seeing it?

A shot is made up of several elements. One of these is **composition**: this has developed into a convention through fine art, photography and film. The more you've been exposed to, the more you will recognize what makes 'good' composition. Essentially composing your frame is you showing the audience what you want to show them. If the location is a bedroom, it's up to you what part of that room we see – whether we look in from the hallway, giving a sense of depth, or secrecy (Figure 4.3a), or whether we are right there, in the room with the action (Figure 4.3b).

camera angle

It is conventional to change the camera angle when you change a shot, if you don't change the angle sufficiently it can look like a 'jump' cut.

A jump cut describes a cut that can confuse or surprise the viewer: it may not be enough of a difference from the previous shot, and therefore look like a bit of the film has dropped out. Typical camera practice states that you shouldn't have less than 30° between two consecutive shots of the same action. However, there are always exceptions to the rule. A situation might arise when you need to shock the viewer – as in a series of quick shots getting closer to the subject. An extreme camera angle means something more dramatic to the audience. A

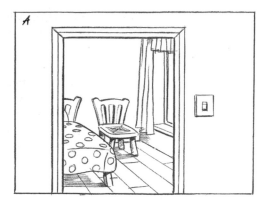
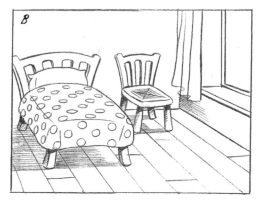

Figure 4.3 (a) Bedroom from hallway. (b) Bedroom interior. Illustration by Tony Guy

low angle makes the character seem bigger, possibly more threatening, whereas looking down on a character makes them seem smaller and less significant. So camera angles bring a lot to the story.

motivation

What is the motivation to cut to another angle, or to cut to another shot? A movement is a motivation to change, it doesn't need to be a large movement, but the viewer is drawn to the movement. If it is the character's eyes looking to the left, we want to see what they are looking at. So the next shot would logically be what they are looking at (see Figure 4.4).

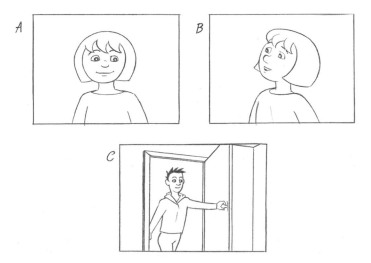

Figure 4.4 (a) M/S Character looking forward. (b) M/S Character looks to left. (c) W/A shot; new character enters from left. Illustration by Tony Guy

continuity

It is important that one shot flows into the next without jumping, and this is helped by the action continuing in the same direction. For instance, if the characters are seen leaving left of stage in one shot and entering the next shot, it is important that they are walking in the same direction for continuity, so they would enter to the right of the stage.

You want to make sure the audience know, even if it is off screen, where the door is, or where the other people are in relationship to the character that's in shot.

crossing the line

This is one of the basic rules that even professionals get wrong, regularly. It is about knowing how characters relate to each other and how the viewer sees them, and the confusion of putting a 3D world onto a 2D screen. If you imagine a conventional set with two characters conversing, the line of the action goes through them, so that if you shoot one character from position 1 and the next from position 2, the other side of the line, the result will be confusing. However, if the camera were to move, or track round from position 1 to position 2 while filming, the viewer would understand the geography of the situation (see Figure 4.5).

reverse angle shots

When you need to see a shot from the reverse angle, e.g. a character is conversing with another, if you angle the shot over character A's shoulder, looking at character B, the reverse angle shot would be looking at character A talking from over character B's shoulder. This kind of shot has an impact on the set – and can mean you may want to make removable walls.

camera move in a shot: (zoom, pan, tilt, track)

This is something I want to bring in at this stage – one needs to think carefully about camera moves. Unless you have a large budget and can afford the equipment necessary for smooth movement, camera moves can be tricky to manage. At least get the camera onto some wheels (e.g. a roller skate with some form of track to keep the camera at the same distance from the subject). Most stories are better told when the camera is unobtrusive. There would need to be motivation for a camera move.

sound

One of the most important elements of a shot is the sound, whether it's actual dialogue or music or sound effects. The sound tells the story as much as the picture, and if something on the screen is creating a sound, then the audience should be able to hear it. You can hear things without seeing them, but you can't see a noise happening without hearing it. So if your character is pouring a cup of tea, we need to hear that tea being poured. Or if the character hears the phone ringing in another room, we do too, and if the next shot is a cut to the other room with the phone in, the phone will be louder in that shot.

Armed with this very basic knowledge, and your own experience as a filmgoer, you can make up a storyboard from your script.

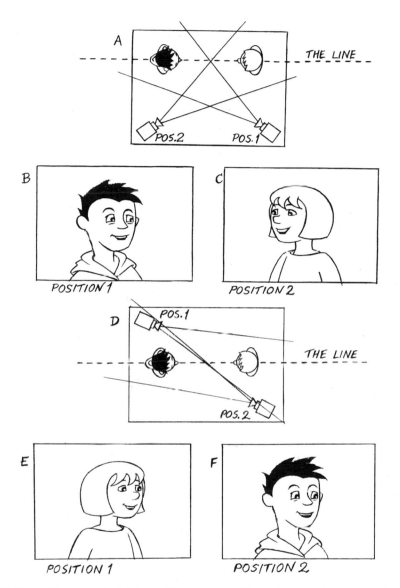

Figure 4.5 (A) Plan of two people talking with camera positions 1 and 2 the same side of the line: (B) shot of character 1, (C) shot of character 2. (D) Plan of two people talking with camera positions 1 and 2 different sides of the line: (E) shot of character 1, (F) shot of character 2 (both looking the same way)

the storyboard

The storyboard is a series of static images, a visual interpretation of your script. Your choice of which images tell the story is the indication of the style of your film. Many beginners I've known are reluctant to plan shots first – they want to get on with animating. But this inevitably lengthens the whole process, which is long and slow enough. If you are storyboarding for yourself, it just needs to be a code you can understand. But generally more people get involved on a production, and you need to be able to explain what is happening. Storyboarding is the most important planning stage of film-making, and the need to communicate your ideas to anyone else involved in the process is paramount. As you realize each image, you need to be thinking about the composition of each shot, the camera angles, and the progression of one shot to the next.

Everyone involved in your film can get information from your storyboard. The set designer can see scale and size of the set, the cameraperson will begin to resource their kit (lenses, tracks, camera height) from the information on your storyboard. Obviously all the details will be discussed as well, but the storyboard is the focus for all these decisions.

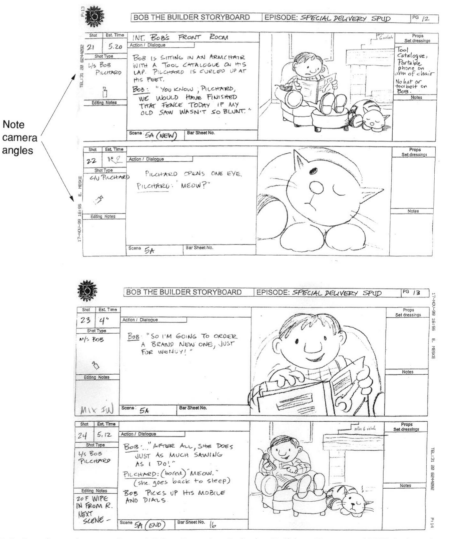

Figure 4.6 Storyboard examples: children's series *Bob the Builder*. Courtesy HOT Animation. © 2003 HIT Entertainment PLC & Keith Chapman

If you are making a storyboard for a whole team of animators, every move, every reaction and every change of attitude should be storyboarded. Proper (not necessarily professional) storyboarding requires knowledge of camera moves and lenses, it requires an understanding of the budgetary limitations of the film and it requires an understanding of film grammar. The professional storyboard artist needs to pick up the nuance of each character. Unless you are doing professional boards, you don't need great drawing skills, although it helps if you have some idea of perspective. The most important thing is to get across the story.

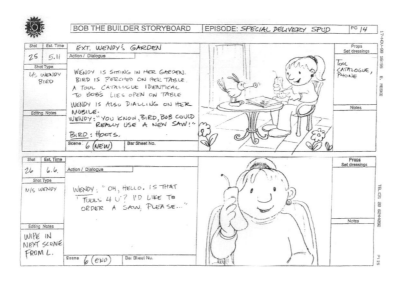

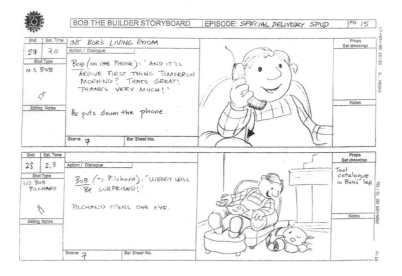

Figure 4.6 continued

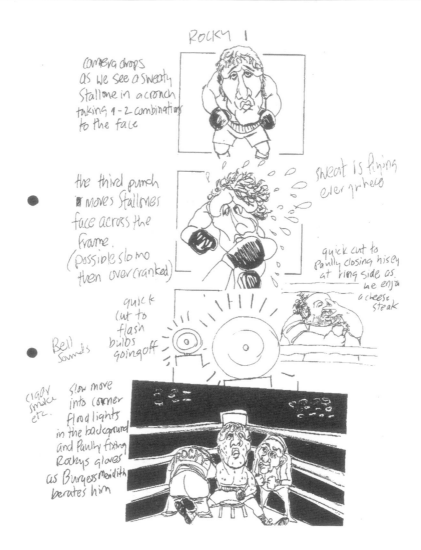

Figure 4.7 Storyboard examples: Brisk Tea commercial *Rocky*. Courtesy Loose Moose Productions. © Brisk Tea/JWT

Storyboards and their accuracy become absolutely vital when work is going to different studios to be completed. The storyboards guarantee uniformity when animation is carried out by several studios, as sometimes happens on a big production, and especially with 2D animation.

visualization

If you are getting development funding, the funding organization will want an idea of the look of the film. Making visuals (a painting or drawing of a whole scene) to go with your script and character designs is important at this stage. Prepare a picture of each scene to

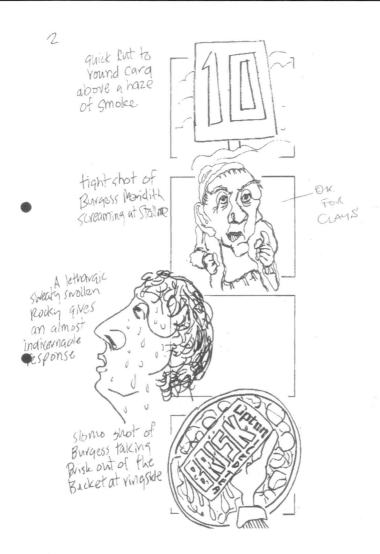

2

quick cut to
round card
above a haze
of smoke

tight shot of
Burgess Meridith
screaming at Stallone

OK
FOR
CLAYS

A lethargic
sweaty swollen
Rocky gives
an almost
indivernable
response

slomo shot of
Burgess taking
Brisk out of the
Bucket at ringside

Figure 4.7 continued

convey the look of your film. The style of your characters and the style of your sets should be coherent.

editing – animatics and story reels

Once you have the whole storyboard done you can edit the storyboard itself, moving pictures around, adding or taking away scenes.

To work out your initial timings it helps to film your storyboard by scanning it into your computer, alternatively use a 2D line tester (this is a video camera on a rostrum, with a feed into your computer). Rough filming like this is called an animatic. This helps you to work out

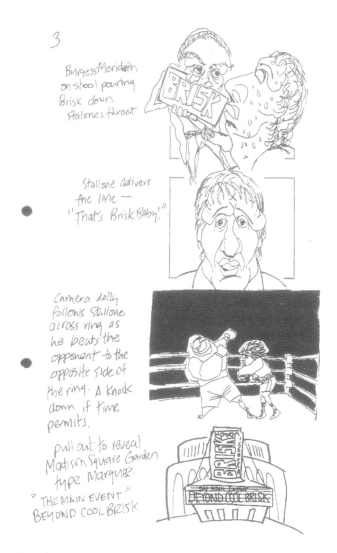

Figure 4.7 continued

your film before you start spending money on sets, voice-overs and model making. In the animation application, hold the image for the timing you've calculated so far. Once you have the storyboard on screen, you can do your first real edit. With animation, unlike live film, the film is planned down to the smallest detail before you start a shot. An experienced editor brings a fresh eye to your production and can see what works and what doesn't. They will implement the principles we have discussed above, edit and make more detailed decisions about the film. This can save you a lot of time and money. It may be that some scenes are actually superfluous in the telling of the story – or maybe you've missed a vital shot that could explain the gag. This is what an editor looks for. An editor can help keep pace in your film, keep tension and rhythm. Be prepared for a lot of cutting and pasting.

If you are going to be using dialogue, this is the time to record a 'scratch' dialogue track. Rather than going to the expense of a professional voice-over and recording at this stage, record yourself or your friends. Depending on your computer, you can record sound directly into it, or if not, record onto a CD. Edit the images to your dialogue track, and if you can, bring in an editor again at this stage to help with the story. Now you are ready to start working out your timings and putting them onto a dope sheet.

If you are working for a client, an animatic becomes an even more important part of pre-testing the animation, as for the first time they begin to see their idea as a moving image. You could use cut-outs for your figures and move them across a background.

From your storyboard and designs you have the basic idea of your set. Before building the set it's a good idea to make sure you know where all the action is going to take place and how it's going to work. The set designers/builders usually make a mock-up of the set in card just for this purpose – then the director and the cinematographer can work out the action, the shots and angles. The rough cut-out figures can be moved around this set until you are sure you have a working plan.

Nowadays directors are beginning to use CAD (computer-aided design) for pre-visualization, so that you can see the how the action is going to work in 3D.

Once you are happy with the script and treatment, and the storyboard just needs tweaking, your characters can be made from model sheets, which we will discuss in chapter 5, and a set can be built (see chapter 7).

chapter 5

coat hangers for armatures – making your own model

chapter summary	• character design
	• working with modelling clays
	• making your own puppet

I really admire all Ray Harryhausen's work. I did try to emulate him when I started with my own home movies. In the attic – I remember making a model dinosaur, which was bendable – wire coat hangers as armatures – I didn't know anything about the right wire or the right rubber, materials or anything. I used foam rubber on the body – but I didn't know what to cover it with – what would make leathery skin – so I used my mum's old nylon tights and spray painted it. I never got to make that movie – I had big plans for it: Live Action/Animation movie – but it never came off.

Nick Park

Practice and experience lead you to your own favourite materials. I hope to give the beginner a basic route toward making their own puppets and some idea of the choices. The puppet used in this book is a relatively cheap example of a professional puppet. It is strong, flexible and versatile and should require a minimum of maintenance. A variety of techniques have been used in making the puppet. There are many simpler ways of making an armature and covering, however, for the purposes of this book, I feel that a naturalistic looking puppet with a natural movement of limbs will be generally more helpful to the beginner.

character design

I very much liked making the puppets for The Pied Piper (Cosgrove Hall Films) which was a film that we tried to do in the style of a Jiri Trnka film. The style of the puppets was very simple, but they had highly articulated armatures, so they could do an enormous range of movements. It had been done in the past, in Czechoslovakia and in Russia, but it was not something that had been seen on British television. For animation at its best, the one character I would choose from all the puppets I've worked on is the Pied Piper himself. He was very light, had a lot of articulation, the spine curved, but the look was very simple. A similar, more recently made puppet that had those qualities was the Periwig Maker from the film of the same name.

Peter Saunders

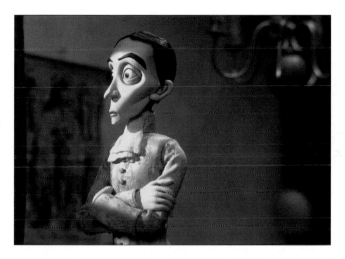

Figure 5.1 *The Periwig Maker.* Courtesy Mackinnon & Saunders. © Ideal Standard Film

Just a few tips on character design – as with everything: keep it simple. Don't be constrained in your ideas by technical considerations, but when you are designing your characters, think about how they will relate to each other in size and style. Only when you have your ideas on paper and you start thinking about materials and structure, might you need to modify them. If you are designing and building your own model, you will need to draw it to scale on graph paper and it is always a good idea to get some advice on feasibility, materials and costs from a professional model making company.

You will need to think of how your character will communicate: is there to be dialogue? If there is how do you intend to animate that? Chapter 8 deals with lip sync (mouth movements in dialogue). You need to decide whether to have a Plasticine head, a head with replacement parts (a removable mouth), or a head armature (skull) incorporating a moveable mouth. Or no mouth at all!

It's very difficult to say what makes a good character. Keep it simple – you can make it as simple as you like – as long as you put eyes in! You do need eyes. Having said that, of course in the Polo ads (commercials made at Aardman), there weren't even eyes! Just polo mints bobbing around – but with a lot of emotion . . . !

Luis Cook, animation director, Aardman

Nick Park developed a wonderful character design with both Wallace and Gromit – with the brow being the device to portray the emotion. Sure, Wallace's mouth is undeniable as a huge part of his face, but the eyes and the brows seem to do all the expressing, and in Gromit's case, being a silent character, they do it all (Figure 5.2).

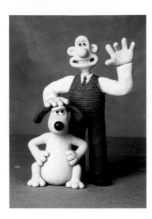

Figure 5.2 Wallace and Gromit. © Aardman/W&G Ltd 1989

The voice you use for your character is as important as the look. Of course, you might choose to work without dialogue and use only sound effects and music, but if you are thinking of a voice, take some time to choose the right one. The voices you choose will help shape your character even more.

You have an idea of the look of your characters, but what of their size, proportions and weight? The scale needs to be decided on for the set at the same time – all the props need to be to scale. What materials would you be making them from? If you go for the cheaper materials, the general rule is that it will be harder to animate. The more expensive the armature, the more responsive the model, the better your animation. Puppets can be made with a combination of materials: wire, clay, foam latex, silicone, wood, resin, leather, fabric, insulation board, polystyrene (styrofoam), fibreglass.

You will want to take the following into account when designing your puppet/model:

1. **How much does it need to bend?**
   This will dictate how strong your armature needs to be; what to make it out of and where the weak points may be.
2. **What's a reasonable scale to work with?**
   The scale for a human figure of average size seems to be about 20–25 cm, although puppets can range from 15–35 cm. If you need to go to close-up it would be worth making something on a bigger scale so that textures look good on camera.
3. **How subtle will the movements need to be?**
   You may need to make or have made a ball and socket armature.

4. **How robust does it need to be?**
   Do you intend to use it for a long film? A series? Will you need to make copies?
5. **How will it stay fixed to the floor for each shot?**
   Do you need tie-downs (screw the foot to the floor to stop it falling over) or magnets and therefore need a perforated steel base for your set? Or are the puppets light enough to just need double-sided sticky tape?
6. **Do all parts need to move?**
   Maybe certain parts of the body could be made with hard materials. Take this into account when preparing moulds.

If you have the funds, you can take your designs to a model making company. If you decide to make your own models it will be a process of trial and error, there are certain rules, but there are just as many new ways to try out and compromises to make. You need common sense, creativity, adaptability, but above all – patience. And by doing it yourself, you will learn a lot more about the animation process.

working with modelling clays

> I tended to steer away from techniques that needed a lot of process – a lot of materials. I think that's ultimately why I went for Plasticine – because there's always room for improvisation, no matter how much you plan it. You've got to have your puppet, you've got to know roughly what'll happen because you need your props and the set. But once you're on that stage you can improvize and change your mind a lot. Some forms of animation demand a lot more planning and then you've got to stick to it. It's like living on the edge – once you've started a shot you've got to keep going to the end. You can't say 'Oh I'll add a few frames there afterwards to slow it down or speed it up.' You've got to be on your toes the whole time.
>
> Nick Park

The earliest use of modelling clay for animation dates from a few years after the invention of motion pictures with James Stuart Blackton's sequence 'Chew Chew Land or The adventures of Dollie and Jim' 1910. In the UK, in the late nineteenth century, William Harbutt invented Plasticine, a modelling clay that didn't dry out, but that couldn't melt either. The original recipe disappeared when the Harbutt's factory closed down a century later, but a similar clay is still manufactured in England.

Creating your character from modelling clay alone is probably the cheapest route for model making, but don't be mistaken into thinking because it's cheap it's simple. It demands skilled handling. Working with clay can certainly give you freedom, but this would have to be balanced by the amount of time needed to re-sculpt, and return to your original shape. It means you have the ability to stretch and distort your figure, unhampered by any armature, but the other side of the coin is the uncontrollability of it. When you are new to the craft it's very easy to lose shape; joints, elbows and knees for instance, can move about disconcertingly. So a character that isn't dependent on sharp edges or definition may be a candidate for clay. Aardman Animation's Morph (Figure 5.3) is made with Plasticine and, as new animators find when they come to attempt animating him, nowhere near as simple as he looks.

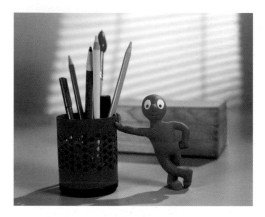

Figure 5.3 Morph. © Aardman Animations Ltd 1995

Plasticine models can be made in a mould. Gumby, Art Clokey's 3D character was originally made with Plasticine rolled out flat and cut-out. From the 1950s onwards they started making moulds, into which they poured melted clay. Now he also has a wire armature (Figure 5.4).

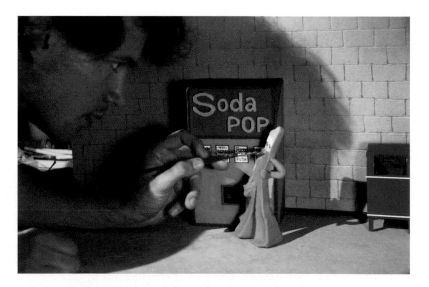

Figure 5.4 Anthony Scott animating Gumby. © Art Clokey

For Plasticine animation there are really very few clays that will do the job. The popular 'English' clay is Lewis' Newplast. These clays have a good colour range, don't melt (which means they handle well under lights), and have a firm sculpting consistency. Van Aken, the US equivalent, has a brighter colour range and will melt and is therefore very useful for moulds, but can get soft under lights. Richard Goleszowski's Rex The Runt, a semi-flat character, is made in a press mould using English clay (see the section on moulds further on in this chapter). This is a relatively fast way of making a replacement character. Rex was filmed against a 45° glass pane, with the background behind, allowing a greater freedom of movement for the characters, a degree of squash and stretch not before seen, and no rigging problems!

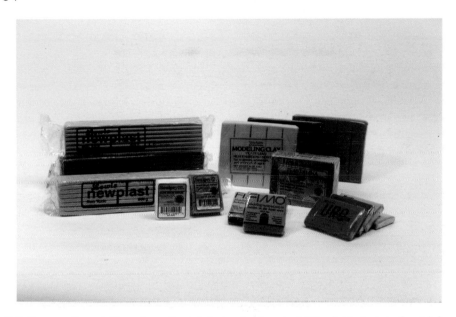

Figure 5.5 Range of modelling clays. Back left: Lewis Newplast ('English' clay), in front left: Sculpey, back right: Van Aken, middle right: Plastalina, front right: Lewis' Uro, front centre: Fimo. Photo © Susannah Shaw. (See glossary, pp. 83–84.)

> *I prefer to animate foam puppets with either replacement faces or mechanical heads. I love the look and feel of clay animation, but the amount of time spent on clean up and smoothing takes away from the flow of the performance.*
> Trey Thomas, animated *James and the Giant Peach* and Sally in
> *Nightmare Before Christmas*

Modelling clay is notoriously difficult to keep clean. Always ensure your hands are clean before handling the material, using wet wipes – make sure you get a wipe that is not too fibrous and lanolin free. Keep your hands clean by rolling the same coloured clay in them, this removes dust and dirt and coats your fingers at the same time. Avoid wearing clothes that 'shed', like mohair.

In hot, sweaty conditions have some talcum powder available, both for your hands and to keep the Plasticine dry. Never try to soften the clay with spirit-based liquids or you'll end up with a sticky, slimy puddle. You can hold it nearer the lights to warm up. Or if the Plasticine is too dry, it can be softened with a little liquid paraffin. You need to be very careful about diluting the clay's intrinsic properties.

A useful way to keep the volume of your model accurate is to have a record of its weight, so that if you are adding or subtracting clay, you are always aware of what it should be.

Don't try sticking arms/legs/tails on to a torso. This will always be a weak point. Your model will be stronger if you tease your shape out of one piece of clay.

making your own puppet

The best way of controlling the model's shape and movement is to give it a skeleton, or armature. A basic armature can be made reasonably cheaply, with wire. The best wire to use is aluminium, which comes in several thicknesses. Twisting two or three strands together in a slow drill can prolong its use. If you can't afford aluminium wire, you could use tin wire, but tin is more springy (has more memory) than aluminium, and will therefore make animation much harder. There are many ways you could choose to design your armature.

If you are making an armature for your puppet, it is best to keep it to the sizes mentioned above. Anything with an armature cannot be made much bigger or smaller because of the sizes of the parts you will be using. Plan your armature by drawing it out. The model described below has been designed with low cost in mind – it's the same model we've used throughout for the animated sequences, so her flexibility is demonstrated. She is made with a variety of materials each dependent on a different model making process. This puppet should cost between £150–£200 to make. In chapter 6 I go into more detail of professional processes; it may be worth referring forward.

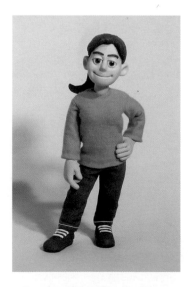

Figure 5.6 Model in relaxed pose. Courtesy ScaryCat Studio

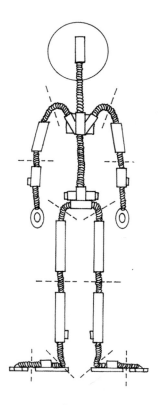

Figure 5.7 Drawing of armature.
Courtesy ScaryCat Studio

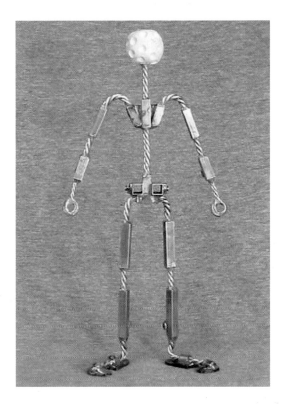

Figure 5.8 Armature.
Courtesy ScaryCat Studio

First of all get three lengths of 1.5mm wire twisted together by holding them in a drill running on slow (Figure 5.9), to make the limbs and the spine and a single strand of 1mm wire for the wrists, looped round a washer for the palm, and twisted. If an armature for Plasticine is too strong, when trying to animate the puppet you will simply poke the wire through. Because of this our puppet only has wire in the wrist and not the fingers. It makes animating the hands a lot easier and less restrictive.

It's always a good idea to be able to remove head, hands and feet, as they often need extra work – so glue on a section of square brass sleeving K&S of sizes that will slot into each other for arms and hands, and head and neck. K&S is square brass tubing that you can buy in any model shop. It comes in different sizes allowing a smaller size to fit into a larger, giving a firm, well-located joint. *(K&S is only available in imperial sizes.)* An M3 nut is soldered onto the larger piece of K&S at the wrist, neck and ankles. This allows the grub screw to be used to hold the smaller size of K&S in place. This in turn holds the wire in place. The strands of wire are then epoxy glued into the relevant pieces of K&S to form the armature. Washers are epoxy glued to the wrist wire to form the palm of the hand.

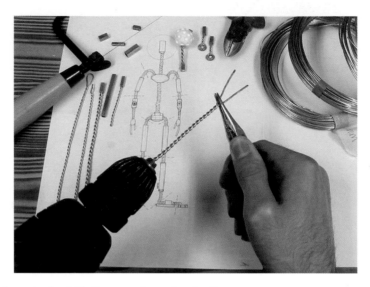

Figure 5.9 Twisting wire in drill. Courtesy ScaryCat Studio

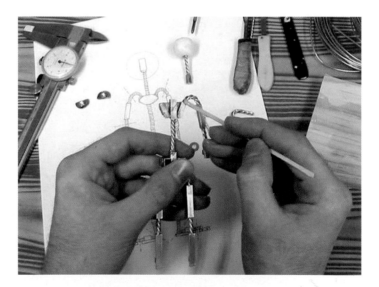

Figure 5.10 Glueing wire armature. Courtesy ScaryCat Studio

To keep definition of the elbows and knees, strengthen the upper and lower arms, and the thighs and calves of the figure by feeding the twisted aluminium through a short length of brass sleeving. Leave enough space for the wire to bend so that the strain is not always on exactly the same spot. Too small a gap between them will make it easier to break.

Steel plate cut with a junior hacksaw is soldered to the three pieces of K&S on chest piece using silver solder.

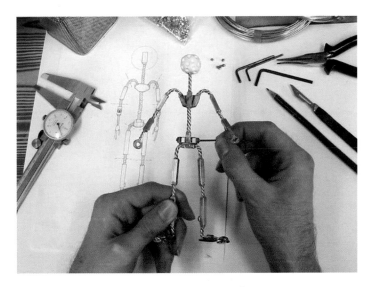

Figure 5.11 Finishing wire armature. Courtesy ScaryCat Studio

head

For the head, it is useful to be able to remove the head and hands for sculpting, leaving the figure in position. It also means less wear and tear to the puppet. So neck joints should have K&S to slot into the head, i.e. $\frac{5}{32}''$ on the neck and $\frac{1}{8}''$ in the head. If you are using a clay head, always model the head with a lightweight core to the rear, to allow for eye sockets and a recessed mouth. Too much clay will make the head heavy. This head core is made with

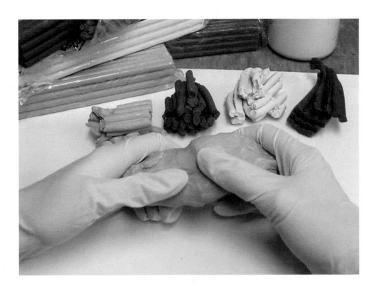

Figure 5.12 Mixing Plasticine. Courtesy ScaryCat Studio

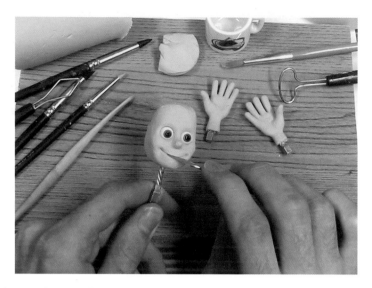

Figure 5.13 Sculpting Plasticine head. Courtesy ScaryCat Studio

textured Milliput, to help the Plasticine 'key' to it. Inside the Milliput head is a piece of K&S for the neck and a piece of K&S for the hair. The head can be removed, as can the hairpiece.

If you are making an animal you might want to add a moveable wire snout and ears to the head core. And if the animal is on all fours, you will need to design it a little differently.

hair

Resin cast hair is useful especially for series work, because the constant removing of the puppet's head to animate its mouth would mess up Plasticine sculpted or theatrical or doll's hair. Our puppet's hair has been made with Milliput, with a Plasticine-covered wire attached for the pony tail (Figures 5.14 and 5.15).

eyes

The easiest way to make eyes is using white glass beads, using the hole as a pupil that can be manipulated with a toothpick. Be careful if you're using a pin or paperclip, as it could scratch off any paint on the eyeball. Painting the irises can be done with a toothpick holding the bead, held by a slowly rotating drill – hold your brush steady and fill in the colour around the hole (Figure 5.16). You can also buy eyes from specialist manufacturers (very expensive) or cast them yourself out of resin.

hands

Hands can be just made with Plasticine on its own, or, if you want to make it stronger, over an armature of fine aluminium twisted wire fingers stuck in a resin 'palm'. Plasticine will allow a fist to bend convincingly, and a firm connection with an object. However, endlessly

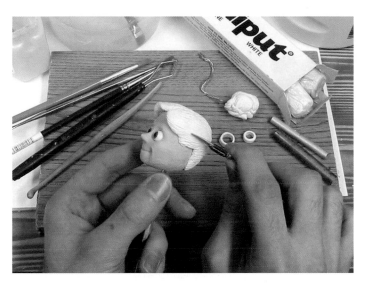

Figure 5.14 Sculpting Milliput hair. Courtesy ScaryCat Studio

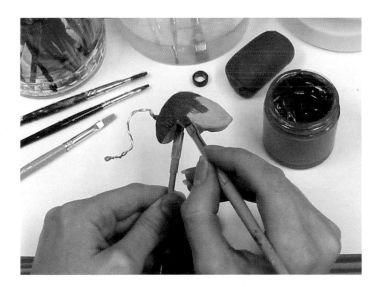

Figure 5.15 Painting hair. Courtesy ScaryCat Studio

having to resculpt and clean fingers is a drawback. An easier alternative may be silicone; however, that can be springy in comparison to Plasticine.

A square brass K&S tube joint is glued or soldered onto the wrist to fit into a tube on the arm. Spare hands are also useful as during filming hands invariably become worn and grubby and if they do have wires, they often break.

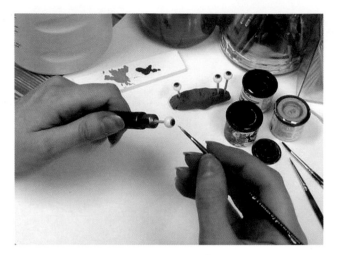

Figure 5.16 Painting an eye. Courtesy ScaryCat Studio

feet

Feet can be made with flat metal plates, or aluminium blocks. It is best to make feet with two plates as a convincing walk is very hard to achieve with a solid, flat foot. Hinged metal plates for your feet can be made with holes drilled in so that the feet can be screwed down to the floor and locked with a wing nut on the under side, or pinned down. This is a slow but reliable method known as 'tie-down'. A more flexible and quicker way of holding feet in place is to use a thin perforated steel table-top with rare-earth magnets under each foot to hold your puppet steady. These magnets are expensive, but very powerful and should be treated with care – they can give you a nasty pinch! Make sure the magnets are kept well away from your computer and video equipment as they can interfere with their magnetic fields.

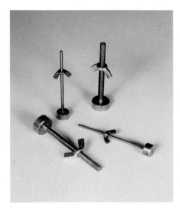

Figure 5.17 Tie-down screws and wing nuts for feet. © John Wright Modelmaking

British animators are, on the whole, more used to working with magnets, while American animators tend to be more used to the tie-down method. Their armatures are made with tighter armature joints making it harder to keep the rest of the puppet still while you move one leg, unless it's firmly tied down.

The shoes for this model are made with silicone: the shoe is first sculpted in a hard Plastiline. To smooth the Plastiline you can use lighter fuel – because Plastiline is much harder than other modelling clays it doesn't get slimy. The sculpt is set into a bed of ordinary potter's clay which will come half way up the boot. The Lego blocks make a wall around the sculpt so that plaster can be poured in and left to set. This will make the top half of the mould.

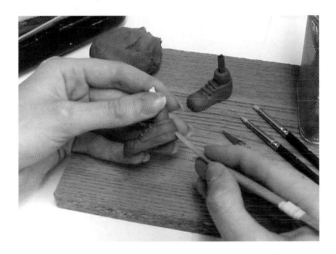

Figure 5.18 Sculpting boots. Courtesy ScaryCat Studio

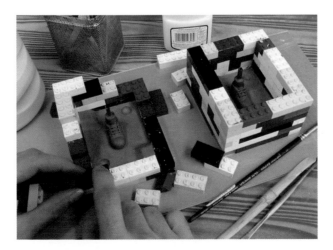

Figure 5.19 Moulding shoes. Courtesy ScaryCat Studio

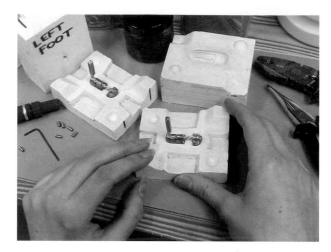

Figure 5.20 Foot armature in mould. Courtesy ScaryCat Studio

The process is then repeated, making a mould for the other half of the boot. Then you will have two halves of a mould into which you can place the foot armature. (See section on mould making for more details about the process.)

Once the two halves of the mould are clamped together, you can pour in the silicone (see chapter 6, section on casting silicone). In this case the model makers have used a coloured silicone. Once the silicone has cured, or set, it can be removed from the mould. There will be a little excess silicone around the joins of the mould – these are called 'flashlines' and will need trimming, either with fine nail scissors, or fine sandpaper (Figure 5.21).

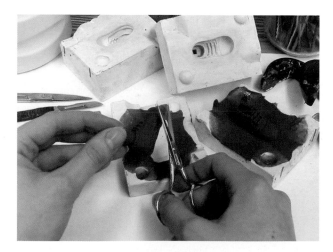

Figure 5.21 Trimming silicone flash. Courtesy ScaryCat Studio

To cover the body, we have chosen snip foam. Other choices could be to cover her fully in Plasticine – a heavy choice; or with foam latex, a process explained in chapter 6. Snip foam is cheap, easily shaped and light. It is basically upholstery foam, snipped into shape and glued on with a contact adhesive.

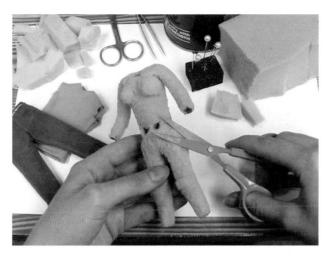

Figure 5.22 Snipping foam. Courtesy ScaryCat Studio

Clothing her involves a hunt for fine-textured fabric that will nevertheless be robust with constant handling. Cat Russ used a fine jersey for her jumper and cotton for her jeans. Once covered with fabric, you have an individual, highly expressive looking puppet.

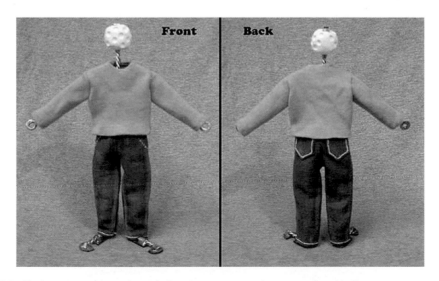

Figure 5.23 Clothes: jumper made with fine jersey cotton, jeans made with fine weave cotton. Courtesy ScaryCat Studio

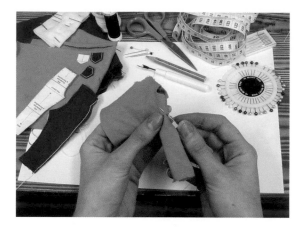

Figure 5.24 Sewing clothing. Courtesy ScaryCat Studio

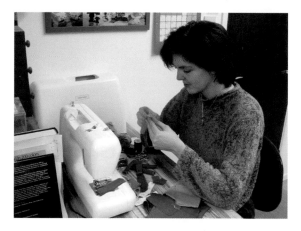

Figure 5.25 Cat Russ sewing. Courtesy ScaryCat Studio

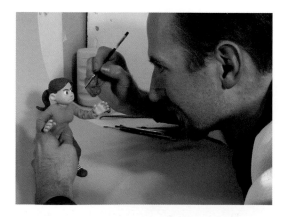

Figure 5.26 Gary Jackson with lively model. Courtesy ScaryCat Studio

list of materials used to make this model

armature

K&S *(square brass tubing, comes in different sizes; we used* $\frac{5}{32}$, $\frac{3}{16}$ & $\frac{7}{32}$ *of square brass K&S tube)*

aluminium wire; *we used 1.5mm and 1mm thicknesses*

epoxy glue	grub screws
steel plate	Milliput
nuts	vice
washers for palms	soldering equipment
jewellery saw	

hands and head

English Plasticine mixed	latex gloves
sculpting tools	

eyes

white beads	paint brushes
enamel paint	

hair

Milliput	paint brushes
acrylic paint	sculpting tools
Plasticine for ponytail	wire for ponytail

shoes

Plastiline	Lego bricks
K&S	paint brushes
clay	Vaseline
plaster	casting silicone
sculpting tools	silicone paint base
silicone pigments	

snip foam

upholstery foam	scissors
Evostick glue	pins

clothes

fabric	sewing equipment
fabric dyes	iron/ironing board
wonder web for pockets	patterns

This puppet would be strong enough to last for a short film. There are many cheaper, and easier ways of making puppets. But in order to practise subtle, naturalistic movement, you will need a puppet at least this strong and flexible.

chapter 6

model makers – the professionals

chapter summary

- *the maquette*
- *ball and socket armature*
- *mould making – hard and soft moulds*
- *casting*
- *colouring*
- *costumes/dressing*
- *glossary of model making materials*

For professional animation, a model making company like the UK's Mackinnon & Saunders work from the animator's sketches and then make a 3D maquette, a blueprint from which they make moulds to make the models. Mackinnon & Saunders started working with Cosgrove Hall Films in Manchester in the 1970s. At Cosgrove Hall, they learned their trade as the company developed and grew. Many techniques we all use today were developed at Cosgrove Hall and many world-class animators such as Paul Berry, Loyd Price, Sue Pugh and Barry Purves learned the ropes there.

Mackinnon & Saunders specialize in models for series work and features, making puppets that are robust and easy to repair with standardized parts to keep them exactly the same all the way through the shoot.

Ian Mackinnon describes the process:

> *A lot of the animators we've worked with over the years have done their own model making as well. People like Jeff Newitt and Ken Lidster from Loosemoose. They would probably make their own puppets if they had time to do it. They like to give us some sort of reference to work from, whether it's a sculpt or a sketch. It's the job of the sculptors then to interpret it and take it from a sketch into 3D form.*

Whilst the sculptors are working on blocking the character out they've got to be conscious of what the job entails from a stylistic point of view. If it's Jeff Newitt's – there's a certain way that he would sculpt a character, similarly with Ken, so we try and mimic that. They would put their stamp on a sculpt even though they're not doing it themselves. The sculptors have to mimic the style so that hopefully, when the costumes and the sets all come together they all look like one complete world.

There might be 6 or 7 different people working on a character at any one stage – its got to go through the mould makers and the armature makers – so to have one (blueprint) model, whether it's painted or whether its blocked out, is useful for everyone to go back to and make sure all the jigsaw puzzle fits together at the end. Also to make sure we've not lost something along the way: the proportions haven't altered because someone's taken a wrong measurement.

the maquette

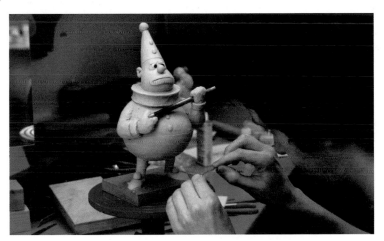

Figure 6.1 Sculptor working on a maquette. Courtesy Mackinnon & Saunders. Photo © Susannah Shaw

With several characters in a story, the model makers will block out all of the characters as maquettes, spending about a day on each one to get the basic proportions. Complications of scale and proportion arise when there are a mix of human, animal and bird characters. These problems can all be ironed out in consultation with the animation director at the maquette stage.

At this stage the sculpt is made over a basic brass sleeve and wire armature, so it can be disassembled, which also helps when you're sculpting it. Little details on the hands and work on the head can be done separately, away from the body; this also makes it easier to finish off. The final materials should be decided on during the sculpting stage. It'll depend very much if the character's got to do lip sync – you might want substitute or replacement mouths. If so, you would choose a hard head. If it's going to be a mechanical mouth, (Mackinnon &

Saunders specialize in mechanical movement inside the head) then it would need to be silicone or foam. Using a mechanical head is a costly process.

All the separated elements then go to the mould making department. The whole process of building up the puppets is dealt with in different departments: sculpting, mould making, casting, painting and armature-making. Once the sculpt is approved, the armature is machined and assembled.

ball and socket armature

A ball and socket armature is more durable and reusable, altogether tougher than a wire armature, and is necessary when a puppet is being made for series or feature work. Apart from its strength, it gives the animator a greater degree of control for finer, smoother movements.

English armatures tend to be made with steel rod and plate construction with ball and socket joints. Joints are made with one or two steel or phosphor bronze ball bearings sandwiched between balanced steel plates. US armature makers use steel rods and ball bearings made with chromed mild steel. The steel balls are annealed (heat treated) to strengthen them. Blair Clark, now a visual effects supervisor at Tippett Studios, was a model maker on Tim Burton's *Nightmare Before Christmas* and recalls 'the animators required joints that could take a great amount of wear and tear. Light scoring on the balls, caused by tightening of the joints, could easily render the armatures unusable. So to prevent constant breakage of the armatures, we made them very strong. I remember the English animators who came over, Loyd Price and Paul Berry, were surprised at how hard they were!'

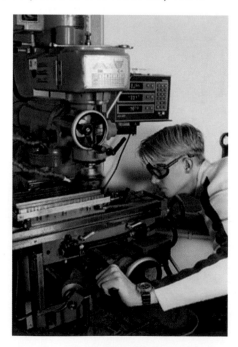

Figure 6.2 Working on a mill. Courtesy John Wright Modelmaking

making your own ball and socket armature

If you are considering making your own ball and socket armatures from scratch, it can be a bit complex, but possible. The cost of the quality of equipment you need to make ball and socket armatures could become prohibitive. Rather than considering buying your own lathe, it may be wise to approach a local art college. A jewellery making department, or even a sculpture department will have all the equipment you need and may relish a challenge.

However, it is much easier to make one up from a kit. You can order all the pieces you need from some model making companies (see appendix 1 for addresses). They can usually supply you with the information you need if you are going to build your own.

Tools that you will need to make up your armature include: a hand blowtorch, pliers and Allen keys. Cheese head, flat head and grub screws are useful. Use silver solder, as soft solder won't solder stainless steel. Don't try using glue for holding your armature together – it will fall apart under any pressure! **Health and safety warning: Take great care using a blowtorch. Use a mask when using silver solder as it releases harmful fumes.**

Good communication is essential when ordering a ready-made armature – so get your dimensions right and use graph paper to draw a plan of your armature (Figure 6.3). It's useful to show the dimensions of the covering material as well. You may know what size and type of joints you want, if you don't it's useful to indicate on the drawing where and how your

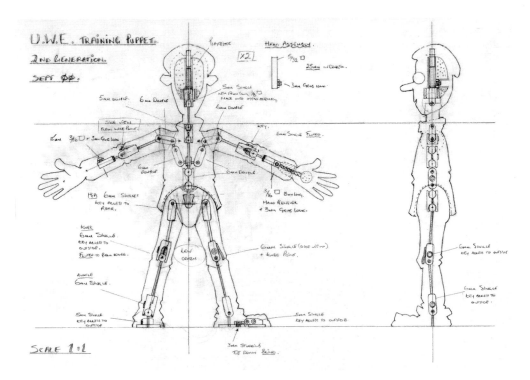

Figure 6.3 Scale drawing for armature. Courtesy John Parsons

character will need to bend. It may be useful to fix a lightweight block of balsa or insulation board on the chest or hip plates, below the covering surface as something for the animator to get hold of, a grabbing point.

Depending on how many limbs your character has, whether it's humanoid, quadruped, or even alien, you should be aware of the way it moves; this will then determine what kind of joints and what size of joints it will have. For instance, the hip joints can have a lot of wear, so you would be better spreading the tension over a double joint at the top of the leg, but you should use a single joint at the elbow to avoid it bending back on itself. Single joints allow for single axis movement, and double joints or full rotation, but beware of double joints folding over onto each other.

humanoid joints

neck: double joint to allow for full rotation
shoulders: 2 × double joints
elbows: single joint, for single plane of movement
waist: double joint
hips: double joint
knees: single joint
ankle: single joint
foot: hinged plate (a single flat plate foot makes walking very difficult)

rigging points

Your character might need to fly or leap through the air in which case it will need a safe point to attach it to a rig. You may want to incorporate a K&S rigging point either on the hips or chest of the puppet. This would slot into a corresponding brass tube on the rig. Or you might want to attach the puppet to wire, in which case you can attach tungsten wire, which is fine and very strong, and almost invisible. Or fine fishing line – this can catch the light a little more – but it can be dulled with wax, blackened with felt tip, or even coloured to match its background. To keep the puppet steady you will want two or more rigging points – the neck and the waist. For professional filming, the safest method is to use a rigging stand, with ball and socket joints; these can be painted out in post production. The reason I mention this is for professional filming is that painting-out a rig in post production is very time-consuming and therefore expensive, and should be avoided as far as possible. Learning to animate with the idea that you can change everything in 'post' is not going to be a very instructive process.

Don't over-tighten joints – never use excessive force manipulating the joints on your puppet, you can easily buckle the plates or rods. Once they are buckled they are very difficult to repair. If you feel that a joint is becoming too loose or too rigid it may be that the Allen key is worn, or that the bolt heads inside are worn which can be worse, as they then become impossible to remove. Use Allen keys of the necessary sizes to make fine adjustments to the joints when necessary. It is useful to keep a drawing showing the joints and which keys are used for which joints, either to save time, or if you have someone else animating your puppets.

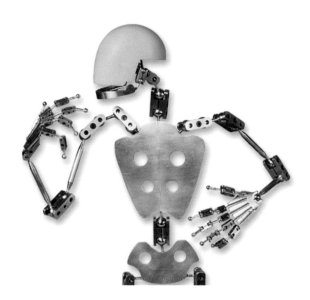

Figure 6.4 (a) Mechanical man armature. © John Wright Modelmaking

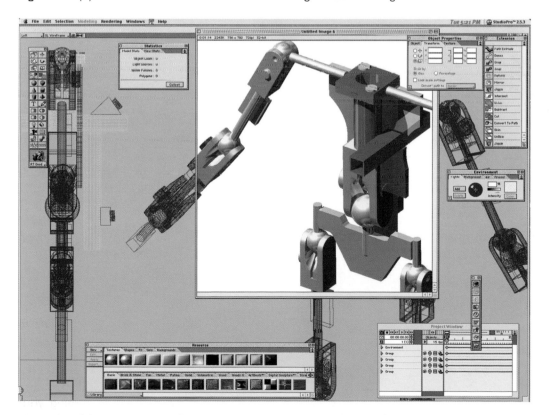

Figure 6.4 (b) Computer aided design (CAD) armature. © John Wright Modelmaking

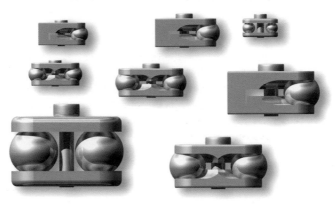

Figure 6.5 Ball and socket pieces. Courtesy John Wright Modelmaking

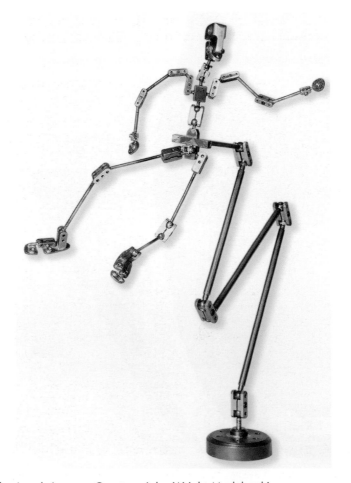

Figure 6.6 Professional rig arm. Courtesy John Wright Modelmaking

mould making – hard and soft moulds

the sculpt

If the puppet is to have a foam latex, or silicone covered body, you will need to first sculpt your model to make a mould to cast these materials in. This is called the sculpt or the maquette. You may also need to make some hard parts for your model: sometimes feet, or hair, or even faces may need to be hard. The general rule is: **If you are casting a hard piece, you will need a soft mould (silicone) and if you're making a soft piece, you'll need a hard mould (plaster, resin or fibreglass).**

Make your armature. You may want to make separate parts of the body that can join together. In this case it's useful on the armature to glue (epoxy) brass sleeve tubing at these points (arms to hands, neck to head).

It's best to use a very firm clay for your maquette, as details and fine lines have to hold as it goes through the foaming or moulding process. Blair Clark, visual effects supervisor at Tippett Studio prefers a Chavant clay. Mackinnon & Saunders in the UK use Harbutts, now made by Newclay Products. Others use Plastiline. Build up the clay and sculpt to the right shape.

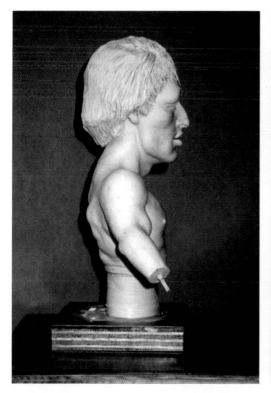 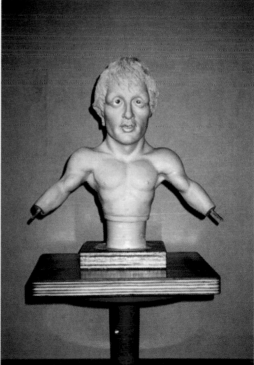

Figure 6.7 *Rocky* maquette made by Mackinnon & Saunders. Courtesy Loose Moose Productions. © Brisk Tea/JWT

Sculptor Stuart Sutcliffe, working at Mackinnon & Saunders, sets a mirror on the other side of the character he is sculpting, so that he can check the figure for symmetry. 'When you look at things, you tend not to see any discrepancies, your eye gets used to it. But with a mirror, the image is reversed, it confuses your brain and you can suddenly see all the discrepancies: there's a big lump on that side, or there's a sharper curve there than the other side.'

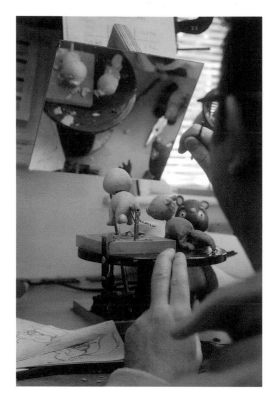

Figure 6.8 Stuart Sutcliffe at work. Courtesy Mackinnon & Saunders. Photo © Susannah Shaw

textures

For textures such as wrinkly skin, dinosaur skin, or fabric you can use ready-bought stamps from various sources or make your own taking latex casts off any surface: old leather, almond stones, bark, leaves, stone. To make good facial wrinkles on Plasticine, cover it first with cling wrap, then mark with a sharp edged tool, it just softens the sharp edges.

undercuts

The presence of undercuts, i.e. a corner or curve that will be problematic when trying to release the mould, is probably one of the most important aspects of mould making. To assess how many pieces you will need for your mould you will need to look the model over very carefully to see if there is an undercut. Don't rush this stage. You will need to work out whether you will need more than two divisions for the mould, and where those divisions should come.

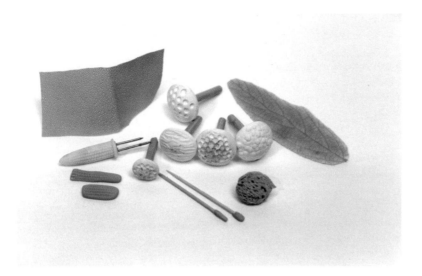

Figure 6.9 Texture stamps. Courtesy John Parsons. Photo © Susannah Shaw

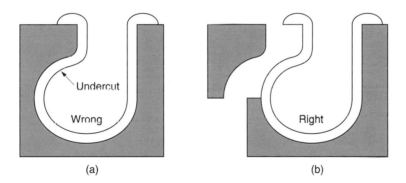

Figure 6.10 The problems of undercut: (a) wrong, (b) correct. © Alec Tiranti Ltd

seams

You will also need to think carefully about where the joins come on your model. This is because when you first take your cast out of the mould, you will inevitably have excess foam or silicone around the join (flashlines) which will need to be cut or sanded away. It would be unfortunate to design your mould so that the seam comes over the face, or some other exposed area. The sides of the body are generally easier to clean up.

The different elements need to be worked out – the body might be cast in foam latex; the head and the hands might be cast in silicone, which means they'll need separate moulds. For maintenance purposes, if it's a series, hands need recasting on a regular basis. Because the wires in the fingers are heavily used, they should have a separate mould so you don't have to cast the whole body each time. The body should only need to be cast once – it should last for a whole series, especially if it's got a costume over it.

(a)

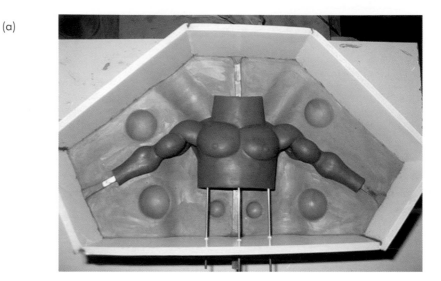

(b)

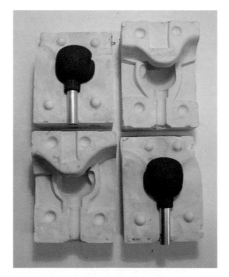

Figure 6.11 (a) Body mould; (b) Glove mould. Courtesy ScaryCat Studio

making a hard mould

Making a plaster or resin (hard) mould for foam latex or silicone:

1. Make a bed of potter's clay or any clay of a different base to your sculpt – potter's clay is water-based and soft enough to bed an oil-based clay (Plastiline, Chavant) sculpt in without spoiling the detail.

2. Build up walls around the bed to the height you need, with card, foamcore or Lego. Lego is versatile, re-usable and can easily be found at car-boot or yard sales. You can build up the walls to whatever height you need.

3. Bed the sculpt into the clay, making sure the clay comes up to your division marks. Ensure that the clay fits exactly around at your mark; it must seal all the way round the model. Cling wrap can be placed underneath the majority of the sculpt before it is embedded in clay. This is to make the clean-up process easier when preparing to make the other parts of the mould. Any creases can be easily touched up on the sculpt.

4. At this stage you also need to make 'key' or location points that will ensure your mould halves fit exactly together. These can be made using small cones of clay, or make a dip with a marble at several points in the clay around your sculpt **(make sure you don't sink the marble any further than the half-way mark, or you'll have an undercut problem!)**.

5. You will also need to put in channels to allow the excess foam latex or silicone to escape when you press the mould together.

plaster moulds

Plaster is cheap, non-toxic and quick. It can crumble if handled a lot. Cristacal or Ultracal is recommended. **Health and safety warning: Ultracal has lime in it – wear gloves when handling. Keep away from eyes.**

To make a plaster mould, brush on your first layer of plaster, this'll ensure plaster has got into every corner. Coat the sculpt with layers of plaster, each coat being added when the previous has become warm. (Plaster warms up as part of the chemical process of hardening.) When cool again, it is set; turn over and take away the clay.

Coat the first half of your mould with a **release agent** – a petroleum jelly like Vaseline is the cheapest and most effective. Then repeat the plastering process over the other half of your sculpt.

If there are more than two parts to the mould (this can depend on the shape of your model), you will need to repeat the process for each part.

resin moulds

- **Fast cast resin** – more expensive, this is a polyurethane-based resin therefore quite toxic, but useful for series work and features as it is very strong.
- **Fibreglass resin (or GRP, glass reinforced plastic)** – uses a catalyst (and an accelerator if required) and is built up in layers with a fibreglass matting. Useful for series work, very durable, but toxic.
- **Epoxy resin mould** – brush on the first layer, and then pour on the remaining resin. Make sure your box is tight, as you won't want resin leaking over your furniture. The resin can be mixed with metal powders such as aluminium for strength, e.g. a two-part 50:50 mix sets in about 5 minutes (depending on type purchased). Consult with the manufacturer.

With these polyurethane-based resins there are certain safety measures you should protect yourself with. Wear a mask to avoid inhaling fumes. Use a barrier cream on your hands as prolonged use can cause dermatitis. Wear goggles

if there is any chance of the resin making contact with your eyes. All the containers should have instructions on them.

making a soft mould

silicone moulds

Silicone is very versatile. As it is so tear-resistant you don't need to worry about undercuts, you can pour the silicone into a containing box, and, once set, release the cast from the mould with one cut and manoeuvre your cast out. Silicone requires a catalyst. It can also be used for Plasticine as a press mould.

plasticine press moulds

Making repeat models in Plasticine can be useful; the Plasticine is built up layer by layer in the mould. Rex the Runt was made with silicone moulds. The silicone is tough and quick to release, making it useful for series work. Fastcast resin or plaster could also be used to make a press mould. For hard press moulds you would need a reliable release agent. Soapy water, washing up liquid or petroleum gel can be painted into the empty mould as a release agent to help remove the Plasticine after it has been pressed into the mould.

There are seven basic rules for mould making:

- For a hard cast, use a soft mould; for a soft cast, use a hard mould.
- Plan your undercuts.
- Think ahead with seams/flashlines.
- Remember to add location/keys to your mould pieces.
- Remember your release agent.
- Remember to block vents – after casting.
- Don't rush!

casting

casting foam latex

Remember to first brush your mould with a release agent (Figure 6.12b).

The basic process for mixing foam latex is:

- foaming up to desired volume at high speed
- de-ammoniation at mid-speed
- refining cell size at low speed
- gelling agent addition.

You will need good ventilation when mixing latex as it gives off ammonia fumes. Depending on temperature, humidity, mixer type and size of the run, this process can take anywhere from 15 to 30 minutes. (Runs smaller than 150 g of latex are not recommended.)

The following two sets of instructions are meant only as a guide and are for 150 g of latex using either the Kenwood Chef mixer widely used in the UK (which has a choice of speeds),

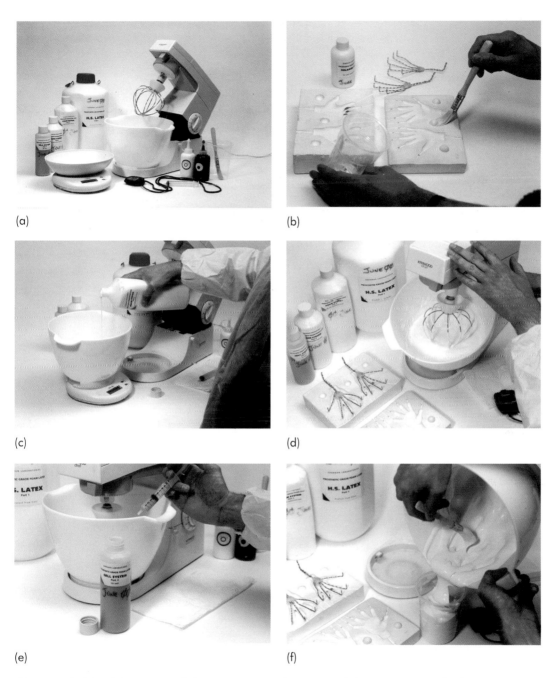

(a)

(b)

(c)

(d)

(e)

(f)

Figure 6.12 (a)–(q) Sequence of photos mixing and casting with latex. Courtesy of John Parsons. Photos © Susannah Shaw

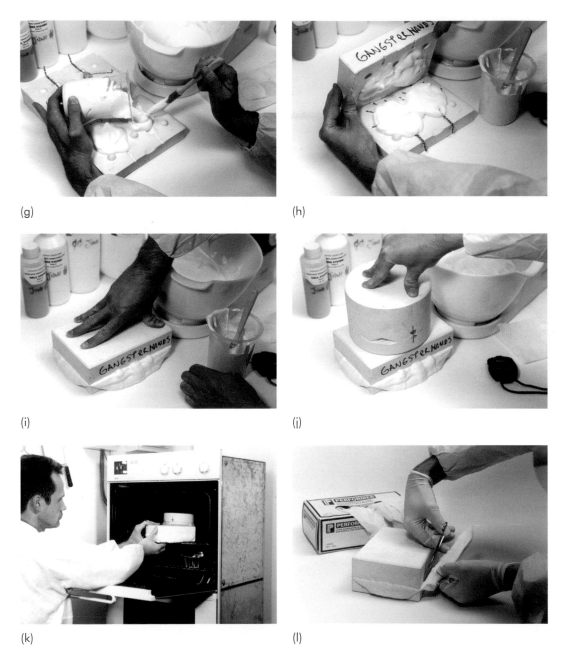

(g)

(h)

(i)

(j)

(k)

(l)

Figure 6.12 continued

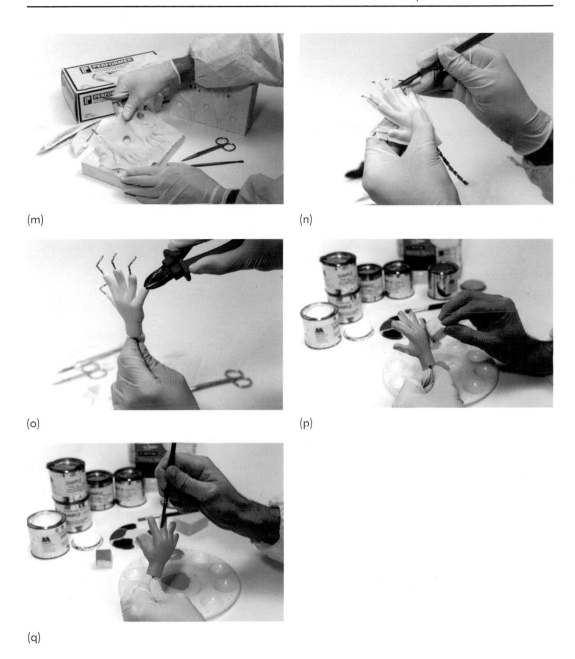

(m)

(n)

(o)

(p)

(q)

Figure 6.12 continued

or the Sunbeam Mixmaster used in the USA, (using the small bowl). The Sunbeam produces a foam of superfine mixture. It has a highly efficient beating action, driving off ammonia very quickly. However, the mixer is less efficient when used in a large bowl.

1. Shake all components well and into the mixing bowl, accurately weigh out:

   - 150 g latex
   - 20–30 g foaming agent
   - 20–30 g curing agent.

2. Foaming – foam at high speed for 3–5 minutes or until the desired volume is reached.
3. De-ammoniation – reduce to medium mix speed for 3–5 mins.
4. Refining – reduce to lowest speed for 5–6 minutes.
5. Gelling agent – at the end of the mixing time add 5–10 ml of gelling agent to the foam. Mix thoroughly for 60–90 secs (the addition of a latex colour at this stage will give an indication as to when the gelling agent is fully mixed in). (The longer times given are recommended as a starting point for 300 g of latex.)
6. Put your armature in place in your mould. The PTFE tape on your armature stops any of the brass from the armature discolouring the latex. Then fill the mould by hand, brushing the latex in to ensure coverage (see Figures 6.12(g)–(j)).
7. Press together two halves and weigh them down or clamp them. Then inject the foam down one of the channels. The injection hole should direct the foam to the core. Let the foam work itself around the whole mould. When you know the latex is coming out of every vent, plug the escape vents with wet clay or English Plasticine (American clay will melt in the oven).

gelling times

The gelling or setting time of the foam at a room temperature of 20°C (68°F) is between 10 and 20 minutes. Longer gelling times may occur and produce perfectly acceptable foams. Faster gelling times can be achieved by slightly increasing the amount of gelling agent, increasing de-ammoniation time. The foam must be set before placing in a hot oven, otherwise foam breakdown could occur. An easy way to test this is to pour left-over foam into a paper cup to a height equivalent to the thickest piece of foam you are casting. Once that has gelled, the foam in the mould should have gelled as well.

curing

When the foam has set (i.e. become a semi-solid easily de-formed material throughout) it may be cured in a suitable oven for 2–3 hours at a temperature of 90–95°C. Curing times may vary depending on the thickness of plaster moulds, etc. You may have to shorten times for fibreglass or epoxy moulds, and increase curing times for thicker moulds or silicone moulds with plaster positives. After curing and allowing sufficient time for the moulds to cool down, remove the foam from the mould and wash. Cured foam is more readily removed from warm, rather than cold moulds (Figure 6.12(l) and (m)).

Plaster absorbs the moisture, generally allowing air to escape, but if you find an air bubble is trapped, more likely if using a resin or a fibreglass mould, you can drill holes in the mould to allow air to escape from likely trapping places. It can take two or three bakes to get a successful cast.

Wash and trim the latex carefully with nail scissors or a scalpel (Figure 6.12(n) and (o)).

care of latex

Latex wears well but will tear under strain. Human sweat will help to rot the latex, so keep hands as clean as possible, using wet wipes. Latex can be repaired with a contact adhesive, coat both surfaces, allow to dry and then press together.

Spirit-based cleaners will dissolve latex during the mixing and airing stages, although once baked, latex is more resistant. As with Plasticine, keep it from becoming tacky with a little talcum powder. Latex doesn't have a very long shelf life; up to six months if stored in ideal conditions. It would make sense to leave buying it until you are absolutely ready for it.

casting silicone

Casting silicone does not involve baking. The main consideration when using it for your puppet is that it is quite resistant (springy) and may reduce the control you have over its movements. One good solution is to cover your armature with ordinary foam   upholstery foam – so that you are only covering a final layer with silicone. That way you will get a reasonable response from your limbs, as well as an easily cleaned puppet.

Once you've mixed your silicone (as per manufacturer's instructions), it is injected into your mould (a large syringe can be bought at a plumber's shop) until it is coming out of the vents. Remember to block any vents with wet clay or English Plasticine, as otherwise the silicone will continue to dribble out.

Leave to cure. Curing times for silicone depend on the type of silicone and how much catalyst is added. On the whole silicone will take about 10–12 hours before it can be removed from the mould.

When set, remove from the mould and clean with isopropyl alcohol. You can sand the seams with fine sandpaper, or remove them using a fine buffing tool with a Dremel or multi tool.

colouring

For latex there are liquid latex paints that can be painted or sprayed on. Before spraying, you will want to 'key' the cast first with liquid latex. The inks can be sponged on and thinned with white spirit. This will cause the latex to wrinkle, but it will settle again.

Water-based acrylic paint like Liquitex can give your foam latex a 'plasticiney' look and has a good opacity and a glossy finish. Acrylics can be mixed with Copydex, or similar latex-based adhesive, to bond well with the latex. For a similar look you can use a water-based gouache.

For resin or silicone pigments, check with the manufacturers for compatible dyes (Figure 6.12(p) and (q)).

costumes/dressing

Many puppets have their clothing sculpted and moulded in foam latex or silicone as part of the whole, but making fabric costumes for your puppets gives them a rich sense of individuality. The most important consideration is the scale of the fabric. You will want to look for prints and textures that suit the scale. If you want a specific pattern, you may print your own fabric.

Nigel Cornford has made costumes for puppets from the early days at Cosgrove Hall: 'If a fabric is too light it is liable to "crawl". In other words, you're aware of the constant movement caused by the animator touching the fabric while filming. In *King Kong* and the early Harryhausen movies, you can see the fur "crawling". So the material has to be stable. I start with a basic white cotton which I dye or screen print and sometimes embroider. That way you can get the scale right. I prefer not to stiffen the fabric, but if it's necessary, if a cloak has to flap in the wind, I'll wire the hem or sometimes I'll stick it to Rosco foil. I prefer to hand stitch costumes for puppets, machining is not versatile enough. I would say, choose the fabric you want, and work your way around it.'

If you're using leather you would want a contact adhesive. If you want a close fit, use fabric cut on the bias, that is cut diagonal to the weave of the material; you will find it gives more flexibility as you stretch it around the puppet. Remember to leave access points for any

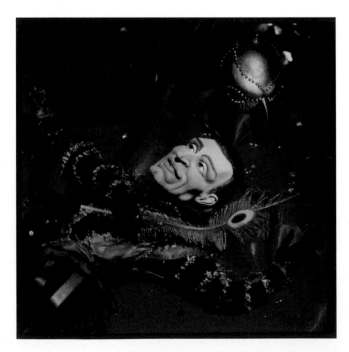

Figure 6.13 Puppet from *Rigoletto*. Wardrobe: Nigel Cornford. © Barry Purves/S4C/BBC

refurbishment of the puppet. It is possible to glue the fabric to a very thin layer of foam to give it manoeuvrability.

For decorating your fabric, pens and fabric dyes are available from craft supply shops. If you are making an additional puppet on a bigger scale, for close-ups, you will need to take the texture and pattern of your fabric into account.

During the model making process it is worth documenting and photographing each stage – there is so much useful information you discover as you experiment, and it is useful to have a reference to processes used. Model making is an under-documented area combining an extraordinary range of skills and as such is always in demand for film and theatre and even medical reconstruction and prosthetics.

glossary of model making materials

For list of manufacturers and outlets see appendix 2.

Allen keys: hexagonal keys available in various sizes, metric and imperial, used for tensioning armatures.

aluminium wire (armature): comes in various thicknesses ranging from 0.5 mm to 10 mm in diameter.

baking oven: must have a low temperature of 50°C showing on the dial.

ball and socket armature: you can order joints, rods and plates from specialist companies.

Chavant clays: a variety of sculpting clay.

contact adhesives: various makes available, e.g. Evostick, useful for sticking many materials.

epoxy glues: very strong glue, a standard 5 minute epoxy is available from hardware and model shops.

insulation board: dense foam that can be carved (available at DIY stores).

Fimo: modelling clay, good range of colours, bakes hard. Used for making props (available at model shops).

foam injector: a large syringe that can be bought at plumbing shops. An icing gun can be used as a substitute.

foam latex: a 'hot' foam, it needs to be baked in the mould. Can be mixed to different densities for different purposes. If mixed fast, it will provide an airier, light foam (used in prosthetics). A slow mix will provide a denser, heavier foam that is good for models and puppets.

food mixer: (Kenwood Chef/Sunbeam Mixmaster) for mixing latex.

glass fibre: used with resin to make very strong moulds. Tendency to warp, so nuts and bolts are recommended to keep parts together when moulding and storing.

Lewis Newplast: Plasticine or English clay has a good colour range (19 colours), colours more subdued than the US Van Aken, and does not melt. Available from model shops and art suppliers in the UK.

Lewis Uro: like Sculpey, similar use (available at model shops).

Milliput: an epoxy putty, also used for making props, white or pink (available at model shops).

Plastiline: comes in two colours: grey or buff. A hard modelling clay, ideal for maquettes for hard or soft moulds. Can be melted or can be made really hard if kept in a fridge.

rare earth magnets: otherwise known as neodymium iron boron magnets. Very powerful and quite expensive magnets to fix your puppets' feet to the floor when using a perforated steel base. From £6.00.

release agents: Vaseline is cheapest and best, must be used judiciously to avoid clogging in corners. Available as sprays and aerosols.

resin: a cold cast product used for making hard parts: hands, feet, and hairpieces. Also used for mould making for silicone or foam casts. Can come with metal powder, i.e. Formite, aluminium powder in resin.

Sculpey: a polymer clay. Available in several types: Original Sculpey, Super Sculpey, Sculpey III, and Premo Sculpey. Must be cooked and cured. Good range of colours (available at model shops).

sculpting tools: used for smoothing, texturing, gouging, shaping clays. People build up a range of tools to their own liking. (Available at model shops and pottery suppliers.)

silicone: makes a rubbery smooth-textured material. It can be cast cold, with no baking required; the colour is fast and can be mixed to match a Pantone reference. It provides a resistant and springy material. Ideal for replacements (substitutes). Very strong, tear-resistant and easy to clean. Good for moulds for resins and Plasticine press.

sticky wax: a removable adhesive material useful for fixing props in place (available at model shops).

Van Aken (Plastalina): fudgy texture, it can get sticky and soft under lights. Has a melting point, which is good for moulding. Colours are saturated but not fast. Good for doing food and when melted, makes a good gloss. Sold in the US.

wood: for bases, blocks, and balsa wood for cores, props, etc.

chapter 7

four walls and a sky – sets and props

research the look

Most of the artistic concepts – the character design and look of your set – are decided before you reach the storyboarding stage, and you will have already thought through the camera angles and lighting scheme. You have probably decided where there will be windows in an interior scene, and what appears outside those windows. This chapter will help nail down some of those decisions.

If your setting is an important part of the story you will want to create the right atmosphere. For your own project, if it's fantasy it's up to you, but for any period or realistic locations do research the look. Get some location pictures of what it should look like: if it's your granny's sitting room, take a photo, decide what is the thing in that room that gives it atmosphere. An old 1950s radio? A pair of slippers? The cat asleep on the back of the sofa? A pile of magazines on the floor? It's probably a combination of all these things. Do you need to be able to see down the street? Does the exterior match the interior? What period is her house?

For a street scene, try to make the angles interesting. Looking straight on from a middle of the road position to a row of terraced houses for a whole scene could be dull. Imagine the viewer looking down on it from a window or from an alleyway across the street. Give your set dimension, add foreground interest: dustbins you can look out from behind. An exterior countryside scene presents many opportunities to create depth with trees or hills and foreground interest with shrubs and bushes.

design and building of sets

In the early planning stages the director and DOP (director of photography) would go through the set design, working out the camera angles, depth-of-field (area that will be in focus) and so on, with the set designers. Then a mock-up of the sets would be made to scale. Some companies use foamcore (two thin cards sandwiching a layer of foam). It's a light and easily cut material, but is an expensive option. Artem, a London-based set and props company, make their mock-up sets with MDF. It's cheap to change, and if the set is approved, it's already made. Stylistically, the set designer will work to the art director, and advise on budgetary restraints that may have to be taken into account.

The DOP will then check the mock-up with a viewfinder to make sure that shots work. At this stage there may be parts of the set the designer knows will not be needed. Allowances should be made for camera angles changing, for lighting and for animator access, and when the set is built it should have walls that can be removed for reverse angle shots (see chapter 4, section on planning your shots).

CAD

Computer-aided design is a useful way of trying out a set first. A virtual set can be built in the computer allowing the 'camera' to fly through, check angles and lenses before committing the budget. Again lighting set-ups can be tried and tested this way, saving on time and manpower. Once the original investment is made in the computing software, the advantages are obvious. However, as with everything done in this way, it leaves no room for the happy accident when you come up with something you wouldn't have thought of, through some external factor. Decent 3D software to allow for the sophistication of fly-throughs and lighting is not going to come cheap and the range includes 3D Studio Max, Lightwave and Alias Studio.

scale

With puppets being around 20 cm to 25 cm, a standard scale to work to is 1:6. The scale of the puppets is dictated by the pieces needed for armatures, and by your depth of field. This is the range of your set that will be in focus. The smaller the scale, the harder it is to give it a sense of depth and without that, you will create a 'miniature' look. If you want your world to look realistic you will need to work at about a 1:6 scale and use plenty of light to give yourself more focal range.

Nick Hilligoss, animator for the Natural History Unit of the Australian Broadcasting Corporation, explains:

> For animation, I do human puppets in about 1:6 scale, so they are around 12" tall. (Some people use 8" tall puppets.) But I also have rats, frogs, and insects, and for close ups of those I make full scale copies of small sections of the 1:6 sets. For wide shots of suburban streets I make 1:24 scale sets. (Because you can buy a

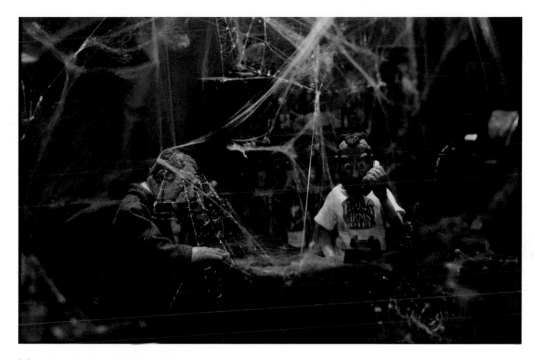

(a)

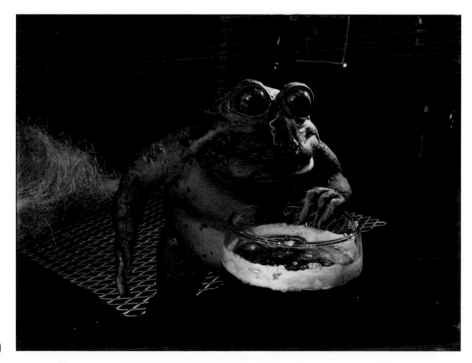

(b)

Figure 7.1 (a) Human puppets at 1:6 scale (© Nick Hilligoss); (b) Full-scale frog puppet (© Nick Hilligoss)

wide range of 1:24 model cars, and they're cheaper than 1:18.) I make 1:24 people for these sets, but they are not meant for seeing up close, they just add life to the shot, and help with continuity of action.

You will need to concentrate on detail if you know something is going to appear in a close-up shot. In some cases, the close-up shot requires a larger scale puppet – and a larger, matching scale portion of the set may be needed.

the base

It's best to build your set at a comfortable working height for animators to get to, and to make it as firm and solid as possible. This may involve screwing things into the floor to fix it, or getting hold of stage weights or sandbags. Glueing table legs to the floor is a more desperate method; another is to use steel trestles, weighted down with sandbags, which have an adjustable height you can clamp your base to.

A solid base made of 12–16mm MDF or plywood means you can fix your puppets' feet with tie-downs, i.e. threaded holes in the feet that can be screwed to the base through a pre-drilled hole using a bolt and wing nut system. You can either drill the holes as you need them, or you could have a pre-planned route. Then fill the holes with a clay that matches your set base. Tie-downs are the best way of ensuring absolute contact with the floor, but can slow the animation up. On a budget shoot, you could use strong flat headed pins covered with matching coloured clay. Or if your puppets are very light, you could use double-sided sticky tape. These won't give you perfect stability, but can speed things up.

If you want to invest in a permanent base, a more expensive choice is a perforated mild steel base. Approx. £100 for 2×1m, 16 gauge thickness with $\frac{1}{8}''$ perforations (with the edges folded over and corners welded). The benefit with this is that you can use magnets under-neath the table to hold your puppet in place. Rare earth (neodymium) magnets provide pretty good stability for animation, as long as the foot area is large enough. Magnets on their own might not be enough to hold a dancer on points, or a large dinosaur with little feet! **Be aware, these are very strong magnets – handle them with care. Never put your magnets near any of the recording equipment as they will play havoc with its magnetic field.** As it is perforated you may use it for screw tie-downs, but if your movements are critical, the perforations might just not be where you want them to be – so if you prefer tie-downs to magnets, use a wood base.

If you are using magnets you want to make sure the covering is no thicker than 1 mm. Christine Walker, production supervisor at Mackinnon & Saunders, remembers her days working at Cosgrove Hall Films:

> *They started off covering the perforated steel sets with sticky-backed plastic sheeting – terrible stuff – put it on and you'd have to sand it a bit and add a bit of texture and then you paint it. Each time you increase the depth between the magnet and the base of the foot, it's critical, because the magnetic draw drops off exponentially. So we came up with covering the sets with tissue, laying water glued tissue very fine, very thin. Then we discovered neodymium (rare earth)*

magnets. We needed them when we had to have texture – grass and snow, as in Pied Piper *and* The Fool of the World. *We had problems with tie-downs because the animators weren't used to using them. On features like* Nightmare Before Christmas *they do several run-throughs and shoot the same scene maybe about 12 times before getting it in the can. The tie-downs are planned. But you don't have that luxury on series work, you're on a very tight budget. So that's why they've always worked with magnets.*

Movement of the set is one of the animator's worst nightmares. Overnight the set may have moved. Check why this is, it may be due to camera movement, or it can be a problem with the frame grabber, or sometimes things within the set have drifted, drooped and flopped. The set can expand and contract with temperature changes. If you can keep the studio at a constant temperature, you will solve a lot of problems. At Christmas Films, a Moscow studio that provided the model animation sequences for *Miracle Maker*, animation happened at floor level. A back-breaking situation for the animators, but the only way they could ensure lack of movement of the set in that studio! Many animators will work through the night to get a shot finished to avoid overnight movement.

creating landscapes

If your character is going to climb up and down hills, jump into puddles, etc. you will need to think of the best way of securing it. But whichever way you choose, it is vital to keep the illusion of weight – and a crack of light showing under your puppet's feet will ruin it.

Nick Hilligoss makes a great many animated films with animals in various habitats:

If the ground's just a little built up, I use longer tie-downs. For monkeys walking on tree branches, I make hollow branches from plaster and fibreglass matting, with no back, so I can put the tie-downs in from behind. It's the same for tree trunks, rocks, hills etc. I make a mound of clay, build the shell over that (like making a mould), then pull out the clay. Then I drill holes and use the same tie-downs. It helps to make up a block like a wooden washer to put on the tie-down, to tighten the wing nut against, so it doesn't dig into the reinforced plaster. If the rock or hill rests on a flat base, I make a hole in the chipboard underneath for access. My puppets have aluminium blocks in the feet, with slots in them for the T-shaped tie-downs. On bare floors I usually fill the tie-down holes with coloured Plasticine. Then it's easy to poke the Plasticine out when pushing the tie-down up from below.

I drill holes in a path beforehand because a drill can shake the set and make sawdust. I drill more holes than I think I need then I fill them with coloured Plasticine. Some sets have a coarse velvet 'carpet' which can have little slits where the holes are, which don't show. And with rough ground, shot from low angle, sometimes the holes don't show anyway.

Landscape textures can be made using sawdust or sand mixed with PVA glue spread over your base paper and painted. Trees can be made with plaster, glass fibre, wood and

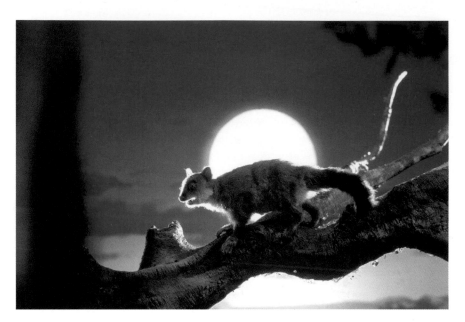

Figure 7.2 *Possum's Rest*. Courtesy Nick Hilligoss

branches. A variety of greenery and foliage can be bought in model shops, but as always, creating your own textures is the key to an individual look.

To create hills and rocks and other irregular surfaces you can use **2-part urethane foam**, a clear liquid and a brown liquid you mix together, which expands into pale brown rigid foam. **(Health and safety note: toxic fumes released when mixing, use outside only wearing a mask.)** The hardened foam is easily carved, but the surface is also easily damaged.

Flocking is another technique that can be used for a multitude of purposes. Flocking creates a velvety texture that is not only useful for close-cut grass, but also for animal skins. It can be added to make slightly longer 'fur'. Using a flocking adhesive, similar to PVA in consistency, coated over the object or area to be flocked, you can go for two basic effects. One is just a case of sprinkling the flock over the area – which gives you a rough finish. Or you can get a smooth, uniform finish that typifies the 'flocked' look and use a flocking gun. This adds a static charge and stands all the fibres on end, giving it a velvety look. For thicker fur this can then be added to. **(Health and safety note: Flock is an artificial fibre, so one should wear a mask to prevent any inhalation.)**

buildings

There are some things for which MDF is the best material to choose: cutting smaller, complicated shapes where you need a clean edge. Buildings appearing at a distance can have detail such as windows and mouldings painted on them. But the closer ones would need the detail added in three dimensions with a reflective window surface put in. Care should be taken that any reflective surfaces don't reflect light or off-set details. Cans of **anti-flare** can be bought at photographic outlets. These cover reflective or shiny areas with a dulling spray. However, because it is easily cleaned off, take care as it can also be easily smeared with finger prints.

For speed, use hot glue. If there are parts of the set that need to be removed for shooting, they can be held together with clamps. Always make sure that nothing has warped, and that edges and corners are true. You don't want a light shining through a badly fitting corner on your set.

interior sets

If there are windows, what is to be seen through them? And if there are curtains, will they be expected to move? Curtains that need to be animated can have thin aluminium wire threaded along the hem. Curtains, rugs or fur can be stiffened with roller blind spray, which is basically a watered-down PVA solution. Alternatively material can be glued to heavy-duty foil.

Any props, furniture, etc. must be fixed so it cannot shift during shooting. Furniture can be hot glued but props that need to be moved about can be temporarily held in place with **sticky wax**, which is less springy than Blu-Tak.

Walls and floors must meet perfectly – again, an illusion can be totally ruined by a crack of light appearing between walls (see Figure 7.3).

practical lights

What's your light source? Are there interior lights? They can enrich the atmosphere and are relatively easy to set up. If it is a night scene are there practical lights to consider: table lamps and such like that will need wiring that need to be concealed? Flashlight bulbs or Christmas tree bulbs are the right sort of size for this. Small 20W halogen reflector bulbs can be used to good effect – with a domestic low voltage lighting transformer that you can buy from a hardware store for about £15 you can control the output of your various small lights.

Lighting can alter the appearance of a set, by creating illusions using shadows such as jail bars or venetian blind shades on a wall. These don't have to be built into the set, you can use a cut-out mask called a 'gobo' and place it in front of a light to create the shadow in the right place. A shadow effect of branches and leaves can be created in the same way, to break up a blank wall or hillside. (See Figure 7.5, page 93.)

exterior sets

Your main light source for an exterior set is the sun or the moon. Either will create shadows. You can choose a general diffuse light with no shadows – but it will give your film more life if you create a natural look that includes shadows. So when painting details such as shadows on buildings, the direction of the light needs to be ascertained in advance.

The backdrop is an important factor in the story. The size of the backdrop depends on the widest shot in the storyboard, and a skilled background painter can create a sense of great distance by use of colour and exaggerating the perspective. If the backdrop represents the

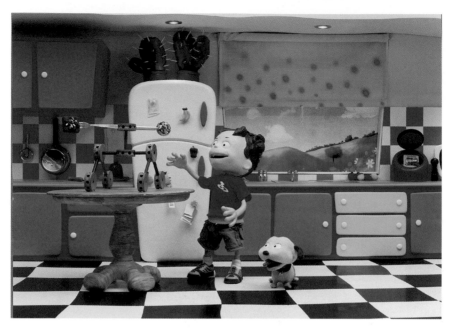

Figure 7.3 Example of an interior set. Puppets, sets and props made by Artem © Bob Thorne, Artem Ltd/commercial for Dairylea Lunchables; OSCAR MAYER is a registered trademark of KF Holdings, Inc. and is used with permission.

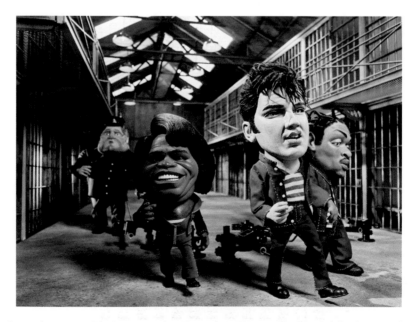

Figure 7.4 Set with practical lighting made using aluminium milled lamp shades and flashlight bulbs. Sets and props made by Artem, puppets made by Mackinnon & Saunders. © Bob Thorne, Artem Ltd/commercial for Brisk Tea/JWT

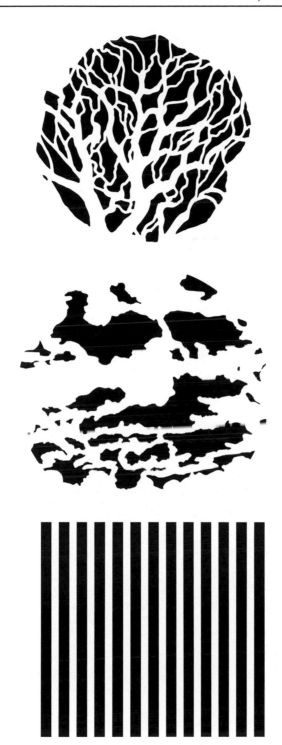

(a)

(b)

(c)

Figure 7.5 Lighting effects: examples of gobos. © DHA Lighting Ltd

sky, it should be lit mainly from below, as the sky is brightest near the horizon. Allow a space between the back of the set and the backdrop for lighting. The 150W halogen 'garage' lamps have a wide throw, but may need a little diffusing as the reflectors in them can cause a 'streaky' effect.

Handle lamps with care: the housings of the higher intensity lamps can get extremely hot. Be aware of the heat generated and the flammability of your set. Don't put any lights too close to the set. The hotter the light the softer any clay animation will become.

forced perspective

There are several ways of creating an impression of depth in your scene. To create a forced perspective, you need a vanishing point – a point on the horizon where all your horizontal lines will meet up. The example in Figure 7.6 has a central vanishing point.

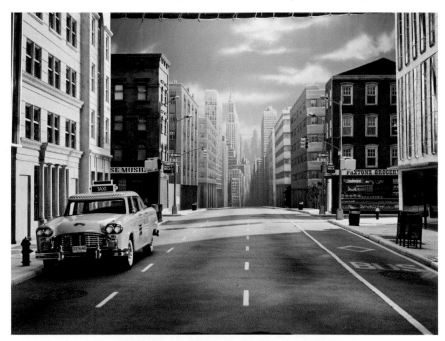

Figure 7.6 Background using forced perspective. © Bob Thorne, Artem Ltd

Place the background/backdrop at a distance from the back of your set if you need the background to be lit from below. The way you paint the backdrop helps to create depth. Distant hills/cityscapes get bluer and hazier the further away they are, a trick of the atmosphere. The sky gets lighter as it meets the horizon, and if you add a bit of yellow to the whitish strip before it meets the horizon, you'll be adding a realistic pollution haze!

If necessary you can make your set as separate strips of landscape, or cityscape, with the details on each strip getting progressively smaller as you go back. If you put a fine spray of white over the trees/buildings, getting denser and bluer the further back you get, that will help the illusion of distance. When using paints, a good reserve amount of the colours mixed should be set aside for repainting and matching.

making props

Prop-making is part of the model making department in an animation studio, as many of the same skills and materials are used. It is dependent on inventiveness and attention to detail.

Milliput, Fimo and Sculpey can all be moulded and baked hard. Model makers all have different feelings as to which materials they use for different purposes. They will collect and horde strange little bits of plastic and metal that will come in handy when making some item or other. Always keep your eyes open at junk sales, toy shops and electrical shops for items that can fit to your working scale. But when you need to get stuff in a hurry there are mail-order catalogues of prop and set building materials.

When making these miniatures, you have to think about your finger prints because a close-up shot will pick them up. Wear latex gloves if you need to.

Insulation board or polystyrene/styrofoam can be shaped with a modelling knife and filed down for less detailed items. Aluminium is good for metal fittings because it can polish up like chrome, and can be cut on a bandsaw and sanded to shape.

Newspapers, leaflets and fabrics can be stuck to heavy-duty foil, making them malleable enough to animate.

rigging

There's a range of mini scaffolding called **Climpex** made by S Murray and Co. They make a series of 13mm rods, connectors and clamps, mostly for use in laboratories but which have also been found useful by photographers and model animators to help prop or hang models and grip things like reflectors and boards. Needless to say it all costs an arm and a leg, but it's worth looking into because it can save a lot of toil and trouble. You should invest in a range of G-clamps along with your tool kit.

Other than Climpex, a scaffolding rig around the set for hanging lights off can also be available for attaching flying rigs. If your puppet is taking its feet off the ground, you can use fishing line or tungsten wire, attached to rigging points on your armature. Give the wire a coat of colour that'll match the background, or keep it matt with candle wax so that it doesn't pick up the light. Using a more sophisticated rigging arm is hard to hide in the filming and time-consuming to wipe out in post production, but is often the solution on a professional shoot.

There are very few rules for set design and prop making, other than the health and safety precautions when using MDF, spraying paint, etc. It's a case of experimenting, trying out different materials, collecting little bits and pieces and hoarding them for when they just

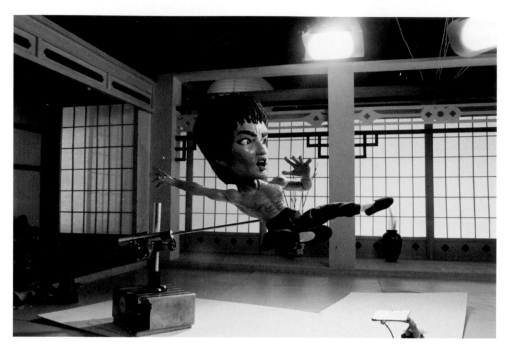

Figure 7.7 Climpex used to make a rig. Set by Artem, model by Mackinnon & Saunders.
© Bob Thorne, Artem Ltd/Brisk Tea/JWT

might come in handy. Hobby shops are a treasure trove of miniature items, but the cost of buying ready-made objects can become exorbitant.

glossary of materials for sets

Climpex: a range of mini-scaffolding, with clamps and accessories with a thousand uses on a set.

Fablon: the original sticky back plastic – available at DIY and stationery shops.

fibre board (MDF): available in most do-it-yourself stores. Dust when cutting is said to be carcinogenic – wearing a mask is essential.

Fimo, Sculpey, Milliput: see glossary chapter 6.

foamcore: a sandwich of set foam between two sheets thin white card, available in different thicknesses, easily cut with a scalpel or modelling knife. Available at art suppliers.

gumstrip: brown paper tape with water-based glue on one side. Available at any stationery shop.

heavy duty foil: Rosco make a black foil, also known as Black Wrap. It can be used for a variety of purposes in lighting such as cutting down spill from a light or flagging off a bit of glare on the lens. Because of its versatility, it has found its way into prop-making as it has no memory, i.e it stays exactly where it's bent, making it useful for curtains, flags or any material that has to move.

perforated steel: a sheet of mild steel with uniform perforations to use as a base for your set, allowing a choice of magnetic fixing or tie-downs for your puppet.

rare earth magnets: see glossary chapter 6.

sticky wax: a removable adhesive material useful for fixing props in place (available at model shops).

See appendix 2 for suppliers.

sound advice

In the late 1970s a new approach was used at the BBC in Bristol (England), when a series was produced by Colin Thomas called *Animated Conversations*. The whole soundtrack was created first. 'Live' dialogue was recorded in a natural setting, like an old folks' home, a pub, or a dentist's surgery. Pete Lord and David Sproxton at Aardman Animations chose a Salvation Army hostel – they then developed characters from this dialogue, and animated to it. Their film *Down and Out* created a lot of interest and the idea was then taken up by Channel 4. Aardman directed a total of ten pieces: the Conversation Pieces and the Lip Sync series. It was for this series that their new animator, Nick Park, made one of his best films, *Creature Comforts*.

A film like Creature Comforts *is much simpler to develop than Wallace and Gromit, because it all comes from the voice track. It all comes naturally from the person who isn't acting or isn't scripted. Because of that it has a certain naturalness that you can only do one thing with. As an animator you listen to the soundtrack again and again, you design the character to fit that voice, then you animate it, very much inspired by what that voice is about. The reason you've chosen that particular voice and that particular section is because it says something naturally to you about what it should be. A good example is the Brazilian jaguar in* Creature Comforts. *The interviewee was talking at the time about student accommodation and the food and the weather here in Britain, he was praising the positive side of living with 'double glazing and things like that'. It suggested he could be a wild cat of some sort, and it fitted with him in a zoo as well. Every time he said 'space', because he kept repeating it, I thought why not use that and work it in as a comedy thing. The soundtrack worked on its own in that film, the characters were so strong that I felt I was just pointing them up really.*

Nick Park

If one is searching for an idea this is a helpful way to get started, and can have wonderful results. It seems a simple exercise to try, but of course relies on the animator developing a good ear for dialogue, recognizing a story, and judicious editing.

pre-production

In chapter 4 we went into the preparation and planning of the visual part of the animation. The sound in animation is almost as important. As with the picture, you have to create the whole world around your characters. Although the majority of the sound design takes place after the animation, recording the dialogue is an essential part of the early production stages.

If you have your idea, your script and want to proceed down that track, you will need to record your dialogue. You know how your characters sound. At this stage, without going to the expense of a professional recording, record a 'scratch' track (a rough sound track of yourself or friends doing the dialogue), either direct onto your computer or onto a CD and edit it to your animatic on the computer. Using the dialogue as your timing, cut your animatic to the dialogue. When you are happy with the timings, you move on to record the actual dialogue.

Once you start to give your character a history, you give it depth and can start to think of the voice he or she would have. Voicing your character is another art. You may have given it a voice yourself, but hiring a professional voice-over is going to make a great difference to the quality of your film. Many actors do voice-overs, these jobs are generally more financially rewarding than most acting jobs, especially if it is for a commercial. They will send a voice reel (a demo tape of their styles), to a voice-over or actor's agency. These agencies can help you to narrow your search if you tell them the kind of thing you are looking for. They will send out demo tapes or CDs. You can also hear the demos on websites, although audio quality over the internet is not always an accurate way of assessing a voice. Most actors, unless they are personalities, will do a free audition, but hiring them for recording is negotiable. Expect to pay anything between £100–£400 for a 1–3 hour session. I can tell you it's worth it. Having heard hundreds of student films voiced by the directors and their friends, to hear one that has been voiced by a professional is a revelation.

Don't feel you have to go for a well-known actor, there are hundreds of actors who've been doing voice-overs for years, whose faces you may not even recognize but who can do the job wonderfully for you. Take note of radio actors especially, who use only their voice.

The actor will want to know as much as possible about your character. Make up a character profile to go with the V/O script, and if you are paying professional rates, make sure you have typed instructions clearly, so as not to waste a moment, but at the same time, don't rush rehearsals. A professional voice-over artist can help you by providing timings in their speech that you may not have thought of and inflections that may change your ideas about the dialogue and therefore the animation.

A good idea, if you've got an actor or actors in to do your voices, is to ask if they mind you filming them. As they are doing the recording they may act out the character and you can pick up a lot of mannerisms and facial actions that will add character to your puppet.

recording dialogue

Lipton Brisk TV
Rocky 1

Open on dramatic combination live action and slow motion sequences. Rocky is being beaten by his opponent. Cameras are flashing. A beautiful girl dissolves through holding a sign that reads the round numbers, etc.
SFX: Punching sounds. Ring sounds. Crowd screaming, Rocky etc.

Announcer: And Rocky Balboa is taking the beating of his life....

Cut to dolly shot directly into Rocky's corner as he sits down. Mickey is all over Rocky as soon as he sits.

Rocky: Who keeps ringing dat bell, I can't concentrate....

Mickey: They should call you the Italian Scallion, cause you stink!

Rocky (barely understandable): You like scallions Mick, Adrian makes a great scallion frittada....

Mickey: He's lost it. Give em' the ice tea, it's our only chance.

Cut to dramatic shot of Lipton Brisk coming out of a bucket. Mickey cracks it open and pours it down Rocky's throat.

Announcer: And Balboa needs a miracle.

Rocky: Ah, That's Brisk, Baby. Hey Mick, when d'you get here?

SFX: Ding!

Mickey: Get in there!!!

Rocky: Classic Stallone Grunting sounds.

Cut to wide shot POV of other fighter as Rocky gets up and comes right at him with an uppercut. We cut to a marquee outside the Spectrum. We hear the punch land and the crowd go wild. Announcer ad lib under.

Title: The Main Event. Beyond Cool. Brisk.

Figure 8.1 Extract from script for a commercial. Courtesy Loose Moose Productions. © Brisk Tea/ JWT

When booking a recording session, discuss your needs first with the company, so as to get the best out of your time.

If you really can't run to the expense of hiring a recording studio, you can do it at home. Try at least to get the best microphone you can afford, and deaden any extraneous noise. You don't want aeroplanes, doors slamming, phones ringing and 'voices off' that have nothing whatever to do with your story. A fridge will make too much of a hum, shoes and chairs squeak. You need a clean sound, so that you can bring in other effects that you want later. A 'dead' room can be created at home by making sure there's no echo. Clapping your hands in the room will show you how 'live' it is, you can hear how much it rings, the sound bouncing off all the hard surfaces. It's best if you have carpet and heavy curtains in your room. Cover up all hard surfaces with pillows and duvets, make sure there's no-one clumping about upstairs, lock the door, unplug the phone – and you will have somewhere to record your voice.

voice techniques

When recording dialogue have the mouth close to the microphone for a fuller and clearer sound; it helps to exclude the room ambience. Too close and you will get 'popping' particularly on the sounding of words beginning with Ps and Bs such as 'presents', 'ping pong' or 'backwards', 'baseball', although you can buy foam 'pop' shields to go on a mic to help prevent this. In fact you can make your own pop shield very effectively with a thick stocking stretched over a coat hanger and placed between the mouth and the mic. It helps diffuse the pops. Differentiating your voices will help: the higher in your throat you 'place' your voice, the more high, or childlike you'll sound; and the lower, the more bass, an older or more threatening character. Already these voices suggest different characters. An older person has more breath or air in their voice. Warm up your voice before recording, by running up and down the range of your voice a few times.

You can record on to your computer if you have a decent sound card, but you still need a good mic. Certain mics are better for dialogue than others, but to make your choice there are websites like **www.shure.com** to help you make your decision. One thing that is always useful to know is how to monitor your audio levels, both for recording and mixing. There are two varieties of meter: VU (volume unit) or PPM (peak program meters). Though both perform the same function, they accomplish the function in very different ways. A VU meter displays the average volume level of an audio signal. A PPM displays the peak volume level of an audio signal. A good analogy that Shure use is that the average height of the Himalayan mountains is 18,000 ft (VU), but Mt. Everest's peak is 29,000+ ft (PPM).

If you are recording digitally it is important that you don't let the meter peak up as far as 0 db (decibels) on a PPM meter – as the resulting sound is horrible. Analogue (tape) recording is more forgiving.

Once you have the recording, you need to break down the sound on a bar chart with each word timed and broken down phonetically, frame by frame (see Figure 8.2).

Alternatively, introducing your dialogue into the computer, using software like MagPie, the sound breakdown process is made very easy. Computer audio packages will give you a waveform – a visual representation of the soundtrack so that you can track exactly, frame by frame, what the mouth movements will be. In the past, when one ran the sound roll back-

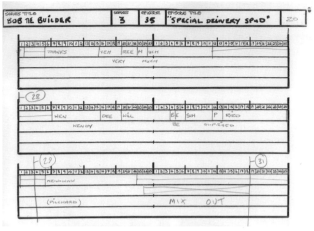

Figure 8.2 Bar chart used in the making of a *Bob the Builder* episode. Courtesy HOT Animation. © 2003 HIT Entertainment PLC & Keith Chapman

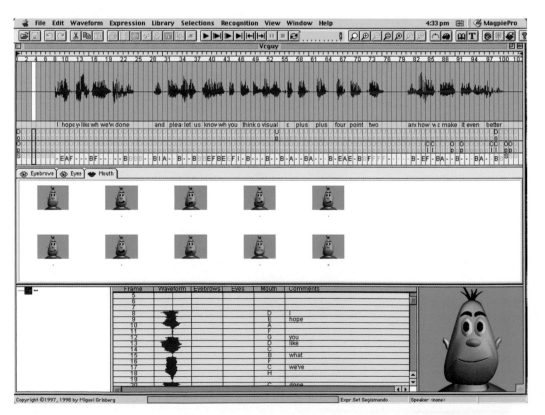

Figure 8.3 Example of a Magpie Pro screen, showing sound breakdown as waveform, frames and a dope sheet. Choice of expressions can be created individually and added to. Courtesy Miguel Grinberg

wards and forwards over the magnetic head, it sometimes took a while to be sure of where the accents hit, but with a waveform you can see to the quarter frame where an accent, or a consonant hits. So as you hear each sound you write the phonetic sounds onto the dope sheet or bar chart.

lip sync

The decision as to how to deal with lip sync needs to be made early on, as part of the character design process. If your character is going to have moving mouth parts, you want to decide whether or to choose:

- full Plasticine head
- metal paddle as part of the head armature giving you an open or closed mouth
- replacement mouth that slots into the head
- whole replacement head.

Lip sync just means the movements the mouth makes when enunciating sounds. However, it is misleading to think that's all there is to dialogue. When someone is talking, the whole face is involved, and not just the face, the whole body is speaking – shoulders hunch, arms gesticulate, hands express. Eyebrows go up and down, cheeks inflate and deflate. Full facial animation is not always easy to take on board with model animation. The extreme move-

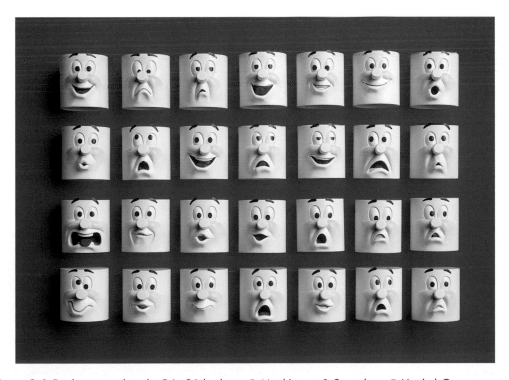

Figure 8.4 Replacement heads. Pritt Stick photo © Mackinnon & Saunders. © Henkel Consumer Adhesives. BDH\TBWA

ments a face can make when happy, hysterical, grief stricken, yawning are all very daunting to think of in terms of constantly re-sculpting a face – how much easier this is to achieve with the flexibility of a pencil.

This is when the skill of the model animator relies more on the tradition of puppeteering, as in the work of the early animators like Jiri Trnka. Use the body of the puppet to express the emotion: use *timing* to express the emotion. Make the face as simple as possible and rely on the mime of your animation to portray the emotion.

Dialogue and therefore lip sync is sometimes better left to a minimum. There are some series when, because of the tight budget, the animators are forced to stick to dialogue-heavy scenes that are low on animation, because the time taken simply to open and shut a paddle mouth is far less than the time taken to express the emotion through the character.

Once you have your character defined, the sort of gestures and mannerisms; how complex its communication will be, will start to emerge. Think through the essential characteristics and pare down, or simplify the range of gestures you will need to tell the story.

In favour of full animation, clay gives you the freedom to create the facial acting to go with the mouth movements. Will Vinton's clay animation on such classics as *The California Raisins*, *The Great Cognito* and the *Adventures of Mark Twain* is a tour de force. Barry Bruce, creative director at Vinton Studios, comments: 'Now much of the animation is done with replacement mouths, it is much snappier, but when we animated with full clay – it was so much more subtle. It is very hard now to find sculptors that are good enough for full animation.'

Nick Park used full facial animation in the early Wallace and Gromit films, *A Grand Day Out* and *The Wrong Trousers*, with Wallace's mouth being gouged out, re-sculpted, and teeth being added or taken away, throughout the dialogue. After that, to speed things up, his characters' faces became replacement from the nose down.

> *Nick's style works immensely well and relies on timing and emphasis. I don't think anyone could lip read Wallace – but the reason it works so well is because it's so emphatic. He tends not to soften things – he tends to jump to dramatic positions, more like old-fashioned drawn animation. When he says 'cheese' it's a huge E, when I say cheese, I bring the lips forward for the 'ch'. Nick wouldn't do that. My best lip sync is 'My Baby Just Cares For Me' by Nina Simone (Aardman made a promotional film for the single in 1987). It wasn't very dramatic, but it was quite accurate. When Nina Simone sings she has a kind of a slur – it's very subtle, but I was pleased with that.*
>
> Pete Lord, Aardman Animations

Bob the Builder™, a typical pre-school children's series character, is designed with practicality of filming in mind. HOT Animation, the studio that produce the series, would not, for instance, be able to produce the 12 seconds of animation a day that is required for a children's series schedule if they gave the characters 'full' lip sync. These puppets have moulded silicone heads over a resin skull with a mouth made with two hinged 'paddles'

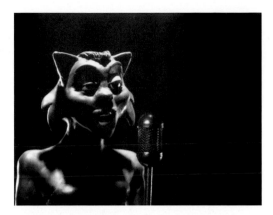

Figure 8.5 Promo for Nina Simone's *My Baby Just Cares For Me.* © Aardman Animations Ltd 1987

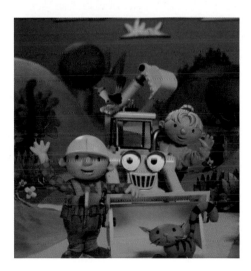

Figure 8.6 *Bob the Builder.* Courtesy HOT Animation. © 2003 HIT Entertainment PLC & Keith Chapman

that can be simply opened or closed. This doesn't allow a range of facial emotions, but means the animators are reliant on their animation skills to make the most of the puppet's body language. The machines have expression change – blinks and eye movement and a range of body language that mean they can shrug and express emotion. Like most children's series work, their puppets have a range of movements suited to the style; some animation is fluid and some dynamic with key poses.

Mackinnon & Saunders, the model makers who make the puppets for Bob the Builder, also made the armatures for *The Wind in the Willows* made by Cosgrove Hall Films. The lip sync for these puppets became more elaborate as the company developed more intricate forms of armature making. They built heads whose cheeks and brows could be articulated under the foam latex covering, allowing a variety of facial expressions. Peter Saunders recalls:

When they were doing the original puppets for Wind in the Willows they wanted the characters to be able to talk realistically. So we came up with the idea of making jointed heads with rubber skins on them, to do mini animatronics. Originally for the one hour special this was used well, but as the budgets progressively reduced for the series, the shots became tighter – they became like talking head shows, and to my mind that's not what animation's about. We created something that went against what we felt strongly about in animation.

Cosgrove Hall has another character, Rotten Ralph, employing another method for lip sync, used in a lot of children's series. Sticking on a drawn replacement mouth as a stylistic approach can work well (see Figure 8.7).

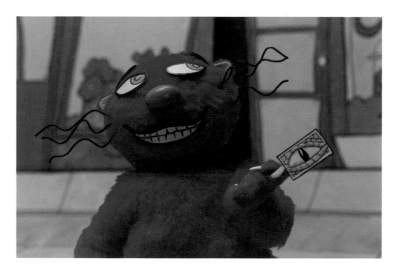

Figure 8.7 *Rotten Ralph* made at Cosgrove Hall Films. © Italtoons UK Ltd 1999 and Tooncan Productions Inc 1999

sound breakdown

The sound is broken down phonetically (how it actually sounds) rather than as it spells. This is so that you can understand what the mouth movement should be for each sound. If you were to break the sound down by the spelling, the resulting animation could well be unintelligible.

The mouth quite often slides from one phrase to the next without punctuating every letter, sometimes moving very little. So unlike much of the other advice you've had about exaggeration keep these moves simple.

a rough guide to mouth shapes: look in the mirror

The following are **suggested** mouth shapes, as are the images that appear on software packages. The 'relaxed' mouth shape also goes between words. The mouth doesn't close between words (or it would look like it was frantically chewing gum); it rests just open.

It depends on who's speaking, but a word like 'Hello' can look stupid with a 'L' shape put in, it may look better if you go from 'he' to 'o'. Or in the phrase 'I love you', you could miss out the 'v' and go from 'lah' to 'yoo'.

Another consideration: Are you going to show teeth? Look at your character, should the upper teeth show when the mouth is open, or the lower teeth – or all the teeth?

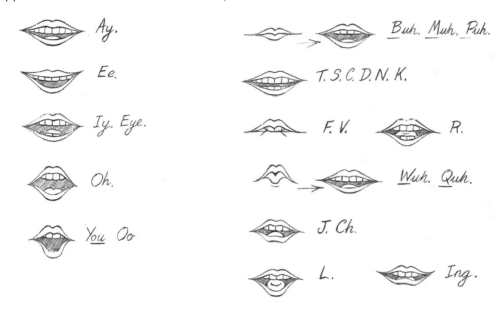

Figure 8.8 Mouth shapes

exercise

Record these phrases and break down the sounds, then animate your model. You could make a bigger head – but it is probably better to try using the puppet you have. Animate the mouth adding teeth or tongue where they are needed. But don't just animate the mouth – frame your shot to show the top half of your puppet so that you can put more feeling into the phrases *and give her character*, don't feel she has to stay female, by taking off the pony tail she could be male.

'Hello'
'I love you.'
'Wait a minute! This is not the way to the airport! Where are you taking me?!'

A word of warning: as with all studio work you don't always have control over the design of the character you're animating. In many cases you are working with a character designed by an illustrator or graphic designer, and have to work out a way round it. Ange Palethorpe, who animated Thunder Pig, a pilot for a series made at Loose Moose, discovered this: 'It was a bit of a shock to begin with. Thunder Pig was drawn by 2D illustrators, the puppet had this huge, heavy snout, which looked terrific on paper, but how to handle the lip sync!? I couldn't change the design, so I had him throwing his head back a lot, so that you could see some movement, but then that seemed to suit his pompous character.'

Lip sync is a very small part of dialogue acting. In any character a lot more than the lips move to tell a story, and it is worth looking at other animated films to see just how important, or unimportant the lip sync is. And to see how much is achieved through body language and sound effects.

> *An animator is like being the actor of the film – we don't design the puppets, they were ready when we started working, the environment was already made, we bring the puppets to life. The dialogue already exists as well, so you have to place the existing dialogue into their mouths and make it theirs.*
>
> Guionne Leroy

chapter 9

the mechanics of movement

I must have been into animation. Even when I was 17 I'd rush home to watch Morph. I loved Morph – Pete (Pete Lord, Aardman) said it hundreds of times – it's the performance. The potential of all this really made an impression on me – it was amazing to be able to tell quite emotional stories through this small scenario on your table-top. And make a proper story that has a tactile reality. Plus you can muck around with lighting and do all your own film-making!

Jeff Newitt

This chapter goes into much more detail about the actual craft of animation, and I am giving you examples taken from observation of natural movement. Once you have a feel for creating natural movement, it becomes easier to create comic movement, and develop comic timing.

studies from observation
using live reference

Your best reference for human movement is yourself. Work with a large mirror, feel the movements you are doing, where are you putting your weight? Which muscles are you using? Which part of you touches the floor/the chair first? How do you pick something up? Get hold of a VHS player with a frame-by-frame viewing function. Make videos of yourself performing actions, study them, time them.

the invaluable Muybridge

A book originally published in the 1880s is still used by animators for reference today: the perennially popular *Animals in Motion*, and *The Human Figure in Motion* by Eadweard Muybridge. The story goes that for a bet, Muybridge, an accomplished Victorian photographer, needed to prove that a trotting horse takes all four hooves off the ground at sometime in the cycle. He set up 25 cameras along a racetrack to take 25 sequential photographs in one second. The result proved conclusively that horses do take all four hooves off the ground at a stage of the trotting sequence. Muybridge then went on to further analysis of human and animal movement, providing us with very clear reference material.

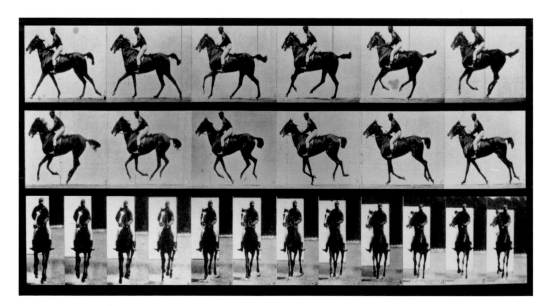

Figure 9.1 Galloping horse. © 1887 Eadweard Muybridge, courtesy of Kingston Museum and Heritage Service, Surrey, UK

When you need to research something specific for your animation, you should view as much material relating to it as you can. This is not to mimic, but to understand. You can pick up characteristics and timings that will add weight to your character. You can look at frame-by-frame analysis of human or animal movement, where you can see the muscles moving, the inclination of the head, mannerisms, all the things that build up a character.

Drawing from life is a very good way to help understand the body and movement. You don't have to be able to draw, but it certainly will improve your drawing if you practice. The idea is that you will really study something if you are trying to draw it. Drawing something in motion is even better, because then you start to understand the 'essence' of the movement. It's a good idea to use charcoal or conte crayon, as you will work in a quicker, looser way, and get a more instinctive feel for it. Many model animators or computer animators shy away from life drawing, but one shouldn't think of it as having to produce a finished artwork. It's merely one way of learning to co-ordinate or link your hand with your eye and brain as an aid to interpret movement. It could involve sketching people or animals in public as you go about your daily business, or attending life-drawing classes at your local college. If this is the case, discuss with the tutor the possibility of doing some fast drawings: 20/30 second poses or 1 minute poses.

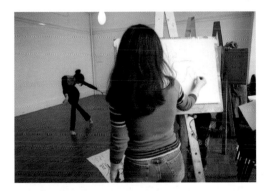
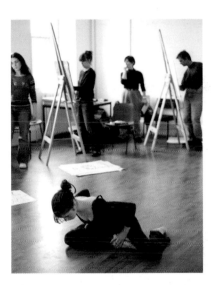

Figure 9.2 Students drawing a moving dancer. © Animated Exeter

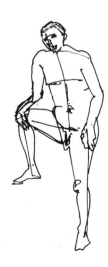
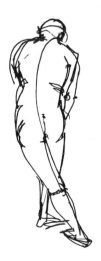

Figure 9.3 Life drawing examples. © Sara Easby 2002

posing the model

Before getting onto more complicated moves get used to putting your puppet into poses, manipulating it into positions that tell a story.

balance

Stand your puppet on the set, then look at it from all round: is the balance equal on both legs? Are the knees bent or straight? If someone is standing straight the knee joint will be 'locked' (unless it's an old character) with the arms hanging. Is the weight all on one leg? If so, the weight of the body should be right over that leg, so that the other leg carries no weight, and is relaxed. Are the arms looking really relaxed? If the arms are relaxed, the elbows will be slightly bent, not held down stiffly. Hands – unless your hands are cast, and in which case they should be cast in a relaxed pose – won't be stiff with the fingers pointing down. Look at your hands when they hang by your side – the fingers curl in toward your body. And most important of all, are the feet flat on the floor? This is important to register your character's weight.

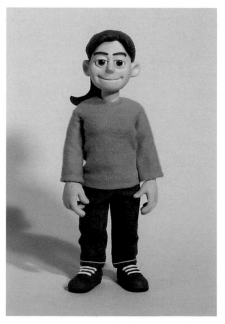 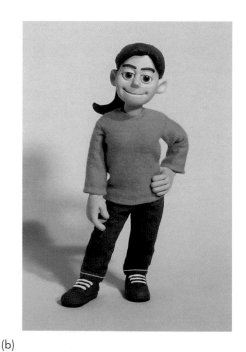

(a)   (b)

Figure 9.4 (a) Puppet posed standing straight – weight evenly balanced. (b) Puppet in relaxed pose – weight on left leg, with left foot centred under body. Courtesy ScaryCat Studio

line of action

Put your puppet in an 'action' pose, hitting a tennis ball, kicking a football or doing the ironing. You might want to make up a few props to help.

Look at your character in its pose from the audience's point of view: does it present a clear image to the camera? Imagine your character in silhouette, just in outline – *then is it clear what your puppet is doing?* If the silhouette is clear and obvious, then the effect will be clear to your audience. The best way to tell a story is with simplicity and clarity, to make the actions stronger than they would be in real life. The silhouette is probably more important in 2D animation, when lines can become confusing, but it's good to think of in 3D in terms of expression.

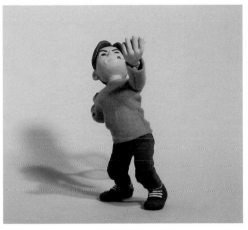
(a)

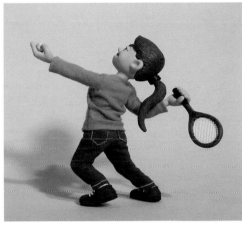
(b)

Figure 9.5 (a) The action is unclear from this position. (b) Same pose from a different angle – this tells the story. Courtesy ScaryCat Studio

Look at the line of movement in your puppet – you should be able to draw a line that indicates where the energy of the movement is. Ask someone else to look at the puppet and tell you what the puppet is saying.

Barry Purves comments:

> It's easy to forget where the camera is when you're animating. It's got to read for the camera, not for you as an animator two inches away looking at it thinking 'Oh this looks good' – look at it from the camera's point of view, because the arrangements of the arms may look ugly and may not read. There's no point doing something the camera can't see. Be aware of the camera; be aware of the framing, be aware of what shot you're coming from and what shot you're going to.

timing

> It always foxes me, timing. I never feel confident enough to tell someone 'just hold that for 16 frames and move on' I can't do that. I'll say 'hold it for just the right amount of time'. Because if you hold it for too long then it looks really stagey and

you've lost all credibility. I remember Chuck Jones talking about rules and I'm so jealous – that would make life so easy.

Pete Lord, Aardman Animations

Although you may start out timing everything with a stop watch, you will begin to develop what in the end becomes an instinctive feel for timing. Because animation is a created process of actions in time, *you are the creator*, you have to calculate how things work in fractions of a second. If something's falling you have to look at the object and assess, by its nature, how fast it will fall and what its impact will be. If someone is throwing something to someone else: how strong is that person, how heavy is the thing they are throwing: how far back will they need to lean to give the impression of the force they are putting into that throw?

The biggest mistake young animators make is assuming timing means live-action timing. It's not! It's not the same timing. You need to emphasize things differently. If someone falls on the floor you need to spend a few more frames developing that weight than you can in live action. Because in model animation we're deprived of blurring the image – you've got to find different ways to address that weight.

Barry Purves

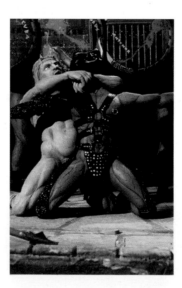

Figure 9.6 From *Achilles* directed by Barry Purves © Barry Purves/C4/Bare Boards Productions

I think my style is all about timing. The timing has to have believability. I plan it roughly, especially with the framestores and playback. I want to go off on little explorations to do with timing. Look for those natural little flicks.

Jeff Newitt

weight

The illusion of weight is created by a combination of observation and timing. Watch a weightlifter tackle a heavy weight. Because what they are doing is so extreme it is useful to study, as an animator. I watched an acrobat setting up her trapeze in a field recently. A slight girl wielding an enormous mallet. She moved very slowly, feeling her way with the weight, and it was that slowness of movement that told of the weight she was moving. She shifted her body to control and counterbalance the weight.

If you haven't observed how a weight is lifted or pushed, you will not be able to create the illusion. And your animation could appear as in Figure 9.7.

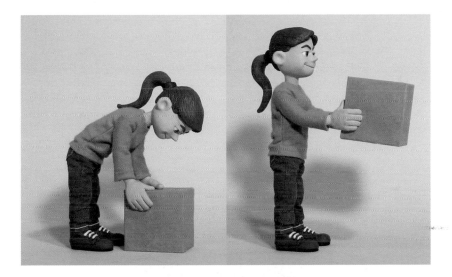

Figure 9.7 How not to animate lifting a weight! Courtesy ScaryCat Studio

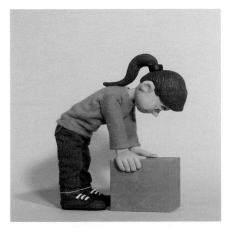

Figure 9.8 Courtesy ScaryCat Studio

In Figure 9.8 the girl looks as though she is leaning on the box, or at least bending over it with no intention of doing anything. Even if she were to lift it up, we would assume the box was made of polystyrene – otherwise she would do terrible damage to her back! The anticipation in this should be the girl conveying *the intention* of picking up a heavy box.

lifting a heavy box

Lifting something heavy needs preparation. You can get more out of this move if, rather than going straight for the bend and lift, you have your puppet study the weight first and then prepare to lift. (*Hold* that anticipation.) Where does the movement start? Practice yourself – you can't very often see just from a videoed performance where a movement starts. You need to *feel* it in yourself. So practice the movement and decide which part of the body leads you into picking up that box? You probably bend at the hip and then the knees. Again the movement is slow – look for the slow and the fast bits. Once you're down (*hold*) – the hands shuffle about to get a good purchase on the box. Not all the body moves at the same pace. In order to get the weight off the ground the body will lean back to get the centre of gravity (the hips) under the weight. Once the weight is lifted, the action is either to stagger around with it and drop it, or to be in control (*hold*), and walk with it. Any walk with that weight will be *slow*, with the weight causing the feet to barely come off the ground.

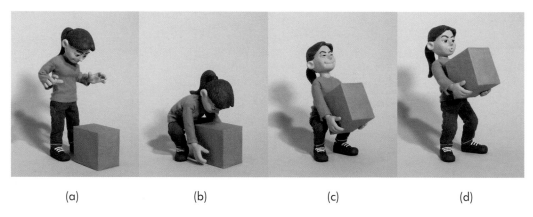

(a)   (b)   (c)   (d)

Figure 9.9 (a) Positions for lifting a weight – anticipation, (b) bend knees taking body right down, (c) lift by tipping body back, (d) success! Courtesy ScaryCat Studio

The illusions you are creating depend very much on the size of the thing that is moving. If it is a small mouse, it will run and scurry about. It wouldn't walk or run at the same speed as a human. Giving it speed in its movements and using single frames will make it seem light and small. The bigger something is, the slower it should move and that will give it the illusion of weight. When filming buildings collapsing on a model set to be mixed with live film, the collapse would be filmed on high-speed cameras making the buildings seem to fall much slower, and therefore giving them a sense of weight and mass.

pushing a weight

Leaning against it, the wall is not offering resistance so much as something that stops the body falling over. Whereas if you are pushing against it, the wall does offer resistance and the body pushes at an angle to the floor while the feet slide back in an attempt to push the body against the wall. The difference between leaning against a wall and pushing against a wall seems obvious, but once again, it is important to get your line of action clear. The poses in Figure 9.10 here are extreme, but her intentions are absolutely clear. It can be easy to go wrong as shown in Figure 9.7 with the box – getting your angles wrong.

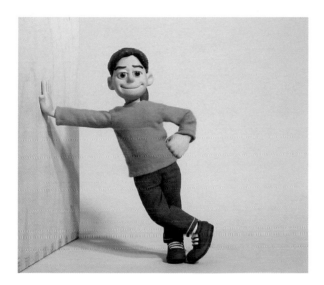

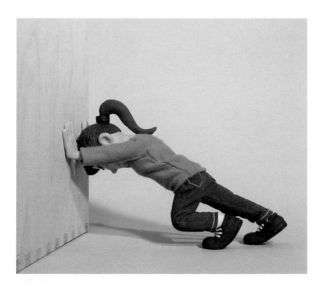

Figure 9.10 Courtesy ScaryCat Studio

A leaf will float to the ground, making no impact on the ground as it lands. A rock, crashing down will either embed itself in the soft ground or shatter on impact with hard rock. A tip here: if you have a very heavy weight falling, you can exaggerate the effect with a bit of camera shake: pan your camera a few increments left and right for one frame each way.

anticipation, action and reaction

Some people say this is what animation is all about: everything boils down to these three words. Before an action there is the anticipation of that action. The anticipation gives weight to the action. An action causes a reaction. Charlie Chaplin is quoted as saying "Tell 'em what you're going to do. Do it. Tell 'em you've done it." Which is another way of saying anticipation, action, reaction. Make it clear!

For example, serving a tennis ball:

- **anticipation**: raise the ball and prepare racquet
- **action:** throw ball and hit
- **reaction:** ball travels – player follows through movement.

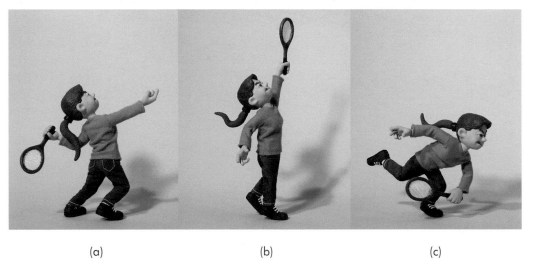

(a)   (b)   (c)

Figure 9.11 (a) Anticipation – preparing to throw ball in the air. (b) Action – hits the ball. (c) Reaction – after hitting the ball, the reaction is the ball travelling, having had the force applied to it, but the reaction of the body is to follow the movement through. Courtesy ScaryCat Studio

Another example: picking up a heavy hammer. The hammer would then be held up for a moment, checking the aim is right (anticipation), then it would come down fast (action), and bounce up after hitting the nail (reaction). This is a recoil movement that is emphasized by the sound (put the sound one frame after the hammer connects with the nail).

To get expression out of the movement, exaggerate it. So the 'hold' when you bring the hammer back would be given a longer time than in real life. Similarly, the reaction after the hammer hits the nail could be more violent, with the piece of wood flying up, or the person's body shaking. These movements take the natural effect and make much more of the reaction.

exercise

Make a video of yourself doing these actions as realistically as possible:

- hammering: a small nail into a piece of wood, the action should be your elbow and wrist working
- lifting a heavy box: using your whole body
- digging a hole in the ground: using your whole body.

Study these movements and break them down into timings. Work out the 'key' positions looking at the line of action.

If you want to try this with your puppet you may want to 'block out' your movements first. Work out the overall time for the movement and divide it up into the key positions. Then shoot each 'key' pose for that time. Once you are confident you have the right positions you can then work out what is needed to get from one pose to the next, keeping the flow of the movement.

The next stage is to get **rhythm and pace** into your movement. It's not just a question of breaking the move down into evenly spaced timings. Each move has its own rhythm:

- **Hammering:** lifting the hammer is a slow movement. The movement starts with the muscles in your shoulder. The elbow works as a hinge, pulling the arm up, with the hand

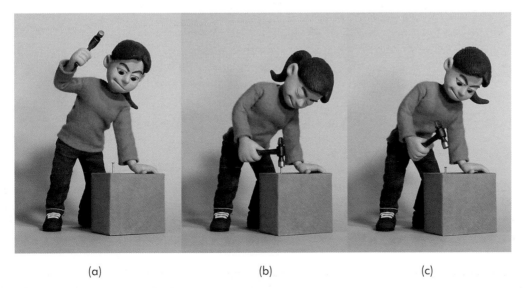

(a)   (b)   (c)

Figure 9.12 (a) Anticipation, (b) action, (c) reaction. Courtesy ScaryCat Studio

following and, last of all, the hammer. The arm will slow down reaching the top until the hand and then the hammer comes up and back over the wrist – note the flexibility of the wrist. This is a key position – *hold* – then the arm comes down fast, dragging the hand and the hammer, and the hand followed by the hammer pivoting over the wrist as the hammer hits the nail – *hold* – and the arm relaxes, bouncing up (with hand and hammer) ready to go back up again. You could hold here unless you are going to carry on.

Digging a hole: In order to thrust the spade into the ground, she will first bring the spade back and up. The back is then bent over to drive the spade into the ground. The hip comes forward to help lift the spade out of the ground, arching the back and bringing the spade up.

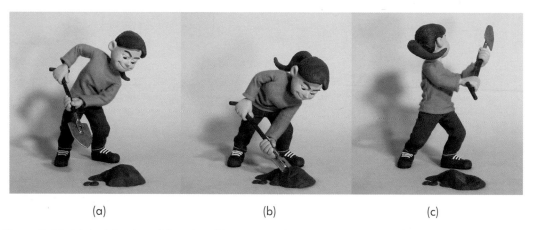

(a)   (b)   (c)

Figure 9.13 (a) Anticipation, (b) action, (c) reaction. Courtesy ScaryCat Studio

● The bigger the movement the more of the body we use. The gardener digging a hole is arching the body back and forth to lever the earth out of the ground – once she has lifted the soil, her body arches back to throw the soil, then the arms swing round and finally the soil flies off the end of the spade. In tennis or cricket, serving the ball or bowling uses the whole body; the energy 'uncoils' from the centre of the body out to the extremity.

You can bring this pattern down to smaller movements. For instance, with hands, if the arms are waving up and down, the movement starts at the shoulder, flexing at the elbow and then the wrist. The hand is the last to move and will flip over the wrist joint when it gets to the top of the move, and then when you bring the arm down, the hand will flip over the wrist joint again – giving fluidity to a movement. If the arm was waving a flag, the movement would originate at the shoulder joint, with the elbow and wrist each acting as a pivot.

One of the most painful things for a musician to watch must be a cartoon violin or cello player animated by someone who hasn't looked. The arm saws stiffly up and down over the instrument. What actually happens is, to keep control and flexibility over their bow, the musician leads the movement with the wrist, rather than 'driving' it from the shoulder.

The wrist is raised as the bow is brought up to the heel and then the wrist drops, pulling the bow back again.

Think of the delicacy of a hand sewing. The same flowing action follows through to the finger tips as the hand lifts and lowers the needle. The wrist raises the hand and the fingers follow and as the wrist drops again, the fingers are reaching the highest point, then they lower following the wrist.

The foot has a rotary movement at the ankle and a hinge at the ball, helped on a walk by having a hinged plate in your armature. The heel hits the ground first, followed by the rest of the foot. When the foot is going to leave the ground to come forward, the heel lifts first. In the same way that the hand follows the wrist, the foot follows the heel.

follow-through

Actions have a natural follow through, like a bowler throwing a ball. These moves are a continuation, a secondary reaction. In other words the main action, as in serving at tennis, is the ball being hit. The follow-through is the arm coming down, the tennis player being carried forward as a consequence of the force used in the action (see Figure 9.11c).

This can be seen in many different situations: in the shake of a head, the hair will follow on after and then settle. When someone stops running, the body doesn't stop all in one go – the body staggers forward, hair and clothes carry on with their own momentum, as far as they can. This is also described as **overlapping action**; not everything in a figure moves or arrives at the same time. When the walk stops, a skirt keeps moving and catches up. If clothing is loose it will follow the limbs later. Usually this is avoided as clothing is made with foam latex or stiffened fabric. But if it is important to the story to have the realistic swish of drapery following the body, the fabric would have to be stiffened on wire or stuck to heavy-duty foil. See chapter 5 on clothing.

snap

There is a point at which too much flexibility and flow in your movements can tend to make everything look rubbery, and the movements all seem to have the same sort of rhythm. This is when you need to know how to give some snap to your animation as well.

For a simple example of getting that impact into your animation, you can go back to chapter 3. In the section on planning, Pete Lord describes a fist slamming into the table to create a convincing illusion of speed, weight and solidity.

Another example that helps to counteract too much rubberiness: when you point your finger, that is an emphatic movement which would be entirely ruined if you kept the same rhythm of movements forward from the elbow through the wrist to the finger. To give this pace, make the finger 'jab' forward fast. To make that jab emphatic take the finger to the end of the move, and then make it go a bit further and bounce back.

breaking up the movement

To make your animation more interesting, break up a move – so that for instance, the whole body doesn't turn at one go, but it turns in sections. So if a person is turning, imagine they are turning because something has caught their interest: first their eyes glance over, followed in a few frames by the head turning, then the shoulders and the rest of the body – almost like an unwinding.

You can reverse that for a different effect. Someone really doesn't want to leave but is being forced to: the hand is being dragged, the body follows but the head is still facing where they want to be, and the very last thing to turn away is the eyes.

walking and running

People aren't choreographed when they move. There may be a natural element to certain movements that on the face of it looks unwieldy, you try to find those natural elements and incorporate them and then it looks right. But to do that – you can't 'think' it – you go looking for it.

I always think that everyone knows how things move, you know when things aren't right. But I suppose it's whether you want to see what's right and wrong. Especially on figurative stuff – just how you shift balance. The main movements are easy enough, but you kind of go searching for those little changes of balance and how that will affect how you'll move an arm. That is what's really fascinating.

Jeff Newitt

Most of the moves above involve weight transferring from one foot to another. In tennis as you serve, you would rock back on your back foot as the body leans back with the racquet – then you will transfer your weight onto the other foot as the arm comes over, hitting the ball. In the digging movement the weight rocks from back foot to front foot. A more elaborate example of weight transference is the walk. Weight transfers from one foot to the other to support the body as it 'falls' forward.

This is where you wish you were doing 2D or computer animation – where life seems safer! Walking a 3D puppet is very difficult – it's what people want to try first, but it needs a lot of practice.

Animators will use many tricks to avoid having to show a walk: a low wall or bushes. There are many ways to avoid showing a walk. In the planning stages decide how crucial to the story is a walk or a run and unless you need to do it, find another way of getting from A to B!

Walking the puppet is difficult. It will shift from side to side, fall over when balanced on one heel. If it's Plasticine, the legs will squash down to become enormous feet – it's *difficult*! The only point at which the balance is evenly distributed is at full stride, with the front heel touching the ground and the back toe about to lift off the ground: the contact position.

rigging

It will be easier to carry out the walk if you can prop your puppet securely. Either keep the puppet upright with something you can disguise, like tungsten wire, or fishing line (you can take the shine off these with candle wax). A prop from the back, avoiding the arm swing, or most securely of all, a rig that is attached to the puppet, holding it upright, that can be wiped in post production. That is the professional and obviously more expensive solution. The rigging point is built into the armature as a K&S brass 'socket' that will take the smaller gauge tube fitting into it (see Figure 9.15).

movement originates from the hip

If you study walks enough you will see that the movement originates from the centre of the body, the hip. The leg is pulled forward from the hip, the body rotates slightly from the hip as each leg comes forward, causing the arms to swing. The arm doesn't lead the leg, and the leg doesn't lead the arm – but, in a relaxed walk, the movement starts at the hip and moves outward – so the hand is the last thing to move forward, as it is at the extremity of the body. You will find moving your puppet by grasping the pelvis and manipulating the legs and body from the hip, means your puppet/armature will keep its shape much better as you walk it. Don't be tempted to pull your character forward by the foot, as the whole shape of the move gets lost.

The full stride is the point at which both feet are touching the floor; the size of this stride is determined by the speed at which your character is walking. And the size of the stride is how you measure the distance your character will cover, and therefore when to bring your character to a halt.

relaxed walk – 16 frames

When you walk the body sways from side to side because the weight is being transferred over one foot and then the other. When the right leg moves forward, the right arm moves back and the left arm moves forward. It's not unusual for beginners to get it wrong and swing the right arm and right leg forward together – I've even seen it on broadcast programmes – it's really a very basic observation. This sixteen-frame walk covers one full step (Figure 9.14, page 124).

fast walk – 8–12 frames (one full step)

In a fast walk the body leans forward more. The weight of the body is ahead of the hips, making the legs move faster to stop the body toppling forward.

In a 10-frame fast walk, the body leans forward, the arms are less relaxed with a bent arm swing; it's an altogether more urgent action with slightly more head up and down tilt.

If any of the walks need to go at singles, try to contrive that the step/contact leg position is straight for two frames, if not, it won't register and one gets a 'Groucho Marx' crouched action.

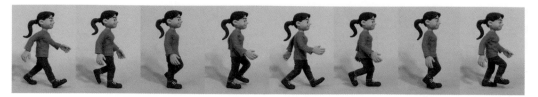

Figure 9.14 Courtesy ScaryCat Studio

run – 6 frames (4 steps per second)

The body leans forward, and the legs fling further forward, the stride is very wide (Figure 9.15). Unless it's a jog, which is a much more up and down movement, with short strides. A run or a jump obviously takes the feet off the ground and you will need to support the puppet either with hanging wires or a rig support. A six-frame run should be shot at singles or the movement won't register properly.

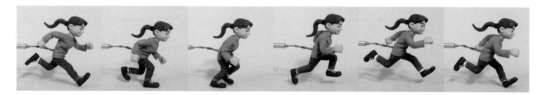

Figure 9.15 Courtesy ScaryCat Studio

Barry Purves' first walk was on the job at Cosgrove Hall Films in Manchester. There was so little model animation being done in England in the 1970s that everyone learnt as they went along, and made up the rules as they went!

> *My first job at Cosgrove Hall was something called 'Grandma Bricks of Swallow Street'. It was a 2 minute soap opera: a street full of characters and this feisty old granny with a dog called Fusby. My first job was to walk her all the way down the street – and I thought 'if I can do this I've got the job!' We didn't have monitors or videos and you could only rarely look through the viewfinder, and when it came back it was all wrong. At first I couldn't see what it was – and then I realised! She was walking toe-heel, toe-heel! Her dog was OK though, he had long hair and you couldn't see his feet!*

the illusion of speed

Moving the puppet or the background while taking the frame to create a blur, known as *go-motion,* is a very effective way of creating a sense of speed. The puppet is normally static – pin sharp when you take the frame. If you were to sprint across the frame in live action everything would be a blur. In model animation you have to work really hard to get those blurs.

- You can blur the background by moving the background when you take a frame.
- You can rig the puppet to the camera, so that they move together.
- Puppets can be on a wire/rig and moved during each frame.

Pete Lord from Aardman Animations observes:

> *Someone like Jeff Newitt will run the puppet over in a chaos of limbs. The knees come very high, arms flap around – it's a jittery effect, but a very energetic effect. Every one of those limbs is a straight line on the screen: the very fact that the lines of the limbs clash and clatter together give an image of frenzied activity and a sense of energy.*

> *A character crossing screen from left to right at speed can look clumsy. One way to get around this is to make a 3D blur in Plasticine. It does look quite ugly, but it works. 1. Make everything as blurred as possible because that gives a compelling illusion of speed and 2. Make everything as frenetic as possible because that gives a different illusion of speed.*

> *Animation is always exaggeration – take the essence of something and then exaggerate it. The human being is so fiendishly clever at putting in the right amount of give in their knees that we barely bounce when we walk. I was looking at sprinters the other day. They are such efficient movers that their legs go like the clappers but the body and head hardly move up and down at all, the line of the head is straight. But if you copy that … it's actually rather disappointing and doesn't look energetic. So the animator should exaggerate the up and down movement to make the effect he or she is after.*

One tip as you get more experienced with walks: If your character is walking/running into shot, start animating off the set: it helps your animation to get into a rhythm, and, if the lighting casts a shadow, the shadow should precede the puppet.

animal and bird movement

The best sources of reference for animal movement are the Muybridge books (see the beginning of the present chapter). Because Muybridge photographed humans and animals against grids we are able to see exactly how far and fast a limb is moving.

four-legged animals

On a walk, most four-legged animals put their feet down front right; back left; front left; back right, as shown in Figure 9.16.

This 12-frame walk can be adapted to most four-legged animals – during a walk the dog/horse/cat will keep two if not three feet on the ground. At a run, as Muybridge proved in his series of horse photos at Palo Alto, a four-legged animal will take all its feet off the ground. Things to note: the tail follows a wave movement and the shoulders will be prominent as the weight of the dog goes over the foot. The legs move asymmetrically, i.e. the front and back legs don't come down on the same frame.

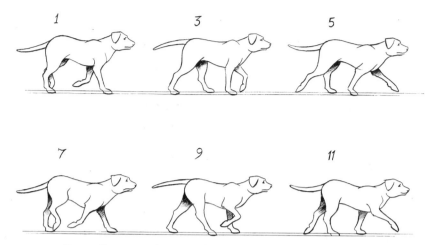

Figure 9.16 Dog walking. Illustration by Tony Guy

lizard

This gives a good example of following a wave movement through a figure – as the body is pulled forward by the front foot, the head turns toward the leading foot creating a wave movement through the body. See Figure 9.17.

birds' walk

A pigeon or a chicken struts, moving its head back and forth (Figure 9.18).

Illustrator Tony Guy, an experienced 2D animator who has worked on many different styles, comic and naturalistic from *Animal Farm* to *Tom and Jerry*, says: 'I have spent many hours over the years trying to work out the relationship between the back and forth head movement and the steps – conclusion? There isn't one! But for animation purposes, throwing the head forward immediately after the step seems to work.'

birds' flight

This illustration serves for most bird flight: for smaller birds such as sparrows, robins or blackbirds, single frame these movements; for larger birds like crows, double frame them. But look carefully at bird flight as the wing movement can differ – a pigeon has a more extreme movement. A bird coming in to land will increase the backward thrust of the wing to brake and come in more vertically to land.

Note: the wing movement will move the bird's body up and down in flight.

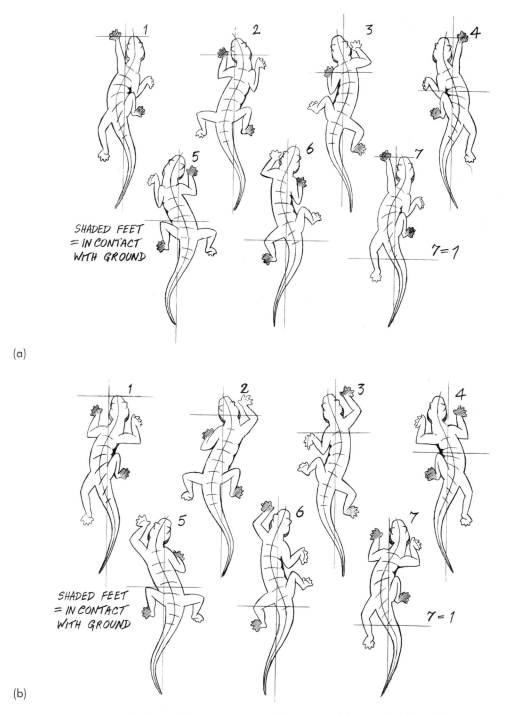

Figure 9.17 (a) Lizard walking: feet in symmetrical positions. (b) Lizard walking: feet in asymmetrical positions – this is the more accurate version, but (a) animates well to give that snake-like movement – and is easier! Illustration by Tony Guy

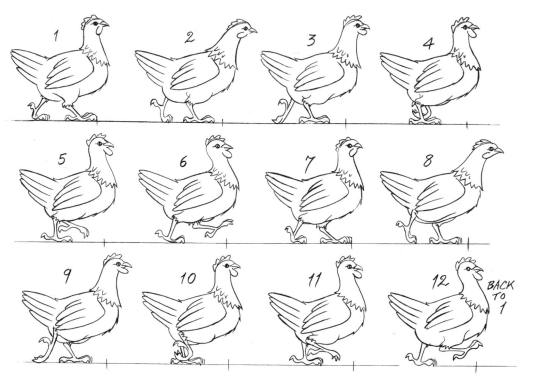

Figure 9.18 Bird walk, chicken, pigeon. Illustration by Tony Guy

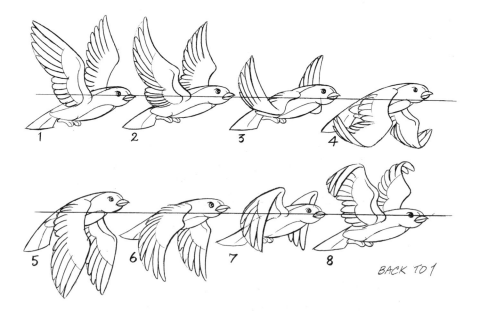

Figure 9.19 Bird flight. Illustration by Tony Guy

chapter 10

the performance

The important thing is performance – and that's not to do with the technique of animation – more to do with acting. Things like performance, timing, sense of comedy, feeling for poses and how to communicate – those are the things that apply across all techniques, and the things that make good animators.

Pete Lord, director, Aardman Animations

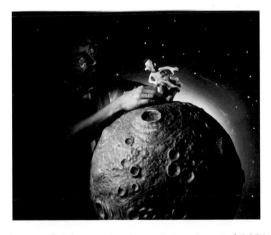

Figure 10.1 Pete Lord on the set of *Adam* © Aardman Animations Ltd 1991

character animation

As animator you are the director and the actor, through your hands this lump of clay becomes a believable character. Whether you are animating a dog, a dinosaur, or a human being, you still have to think about timing, expression, pose, silhouette, lines of action and choreography. You don't need to be an actor, but you need to know about the process of acting, about what reads with an audience.

> *It's very close to how actors think. I learned a lot from reading books about acting. Like Stanislawsky. I think I learnt from reading actors' books but mainly watching, watching, watching.*
>
> Guionne Leroy

Guionne worked on *Toy Story*, *Nightmare Before Christmas* and *Chicken Run*. Her advice is pertinent to any beginner, and you should think about acting as a necessary skill to study in order to develop your animation. Although most animators would rather die than perform on stage themselves, they need to understand the process in order to translate the drama into their characters.

Jeff Newitt (animator on *Monkeybone*) explains:

> *I like the idea of being thought of as an actor. When I went to the States, they almost treat you as an actor, it really felt good. When Henry (Selick, director of Nightmare Before Christmas, James and the Giant Peach and Monkeybone) would go through a scene, he would be going through the motivation, and then when you'd go through testing the shot you were encouraged to go for the performance and bring something to it. Then after the first test, talk about what elements were working. You felt as though you really were bringing something to it.*

Performance is at the heart of good animation. Your characters are actors that have to perform, and as the animator you need to understand how to perform. If your character is to be angry, morose, cocky, or sensitive you first tend to think of the stereotype poses or movements for those characteristics. The good thing about a stereotype is that everyone recognizes it. And as you are in the business of getting your ideas across to an audience, using stereotyped characteristics is not a bad thing.

If you go back to the idea of animating an inanimate object or giving a character to a teaspoon or a matchbox, you have found it is quite difficult to do, without sound effects and without dressing it up. The skill in all character acting derives from mime. This silent art form has been admired by many as being the ultimate achievement in performance art. Even if an actor or a comedian has dialogue, they won't achieve the same effect unless they use persuasive body language. The reason so many of the great animated films have no dialogue is that the great skill of the animator is dealing in mime or body language, so films can be enjoyed internationally (e.g. Michael Dudok de Wit's *The Monk and the Fish* and *Father and Daughter*).

exercise

The story's going to be told by a series of little moments – and it's the order in which you put those moments, those gestures that make the story. For instance, you want a guy to slump in an armchair in a depressed way – you've got the idea of how it should look – but can you do it cleverly, persuasively, humorously, believably? That's what all animators aim for. It's funny to talk about because the difference between good and bad is quite small. It's obvious when it's technically crude, but the difference between a good performance and a bad performance is very hard to define.

Pete Lord

A well-known first exercise for character is to animate a flour sack. It's a very simple shape, and it's also a recognizably inanimate object. The point of this exercise is to be able to put life, to put character, into this little sack. It has a relatively amorphous shape, but the volume of the shape must remain uniform. This is a very important point when working with Plasticine as it's risky to adjust the volume by adding Plasticine or taking it away; you can lose the identity by changing the volume.

So as with Pete Lord's quote about the depressed man, can you make this flour sack act through various different emotions? Because if you can do it cleverly, persuasively, humorously, believably – then you have a little character that you have created.

Using Plasticine, make yourself a flour sack, with four sharp corners that can be used expressively, and go through a few emotions: perky, angry, dejected. Think it into the little sack. Bounce the sack on, or, if it's depressed, have the sack shuffle on, using some of the timings you've learned from the bouncing ball in chapter 3. It's always good to get back to original exercises, as you will find they help to answer some problems you get stuck on.

Keep it simple. Keep it economical. Some animators want to give you fancy stuff but it gets fudgy and messy. Instead of four gestures you can do one really important gesture. Let it breathe – let it have time! Do your homework and plot out the pauses.

Do dance training, go to the ballet – see how a dancer will hold a move – let it read, and then move on. Listen to music, the way a tune is developed and the breath before the next idea comes in. Look at sculpture – the way a story is told just from a single image from different perspectives. I think it's just getting this absolute clarity about what a gesture's about – what a pose is about – and don't ruin it by rushing on to the next one.

Barry Purves

The voices of experience all have the same message, but of course, it's easier said than done. The more experienced you are, the more you will understand what keeping it simple

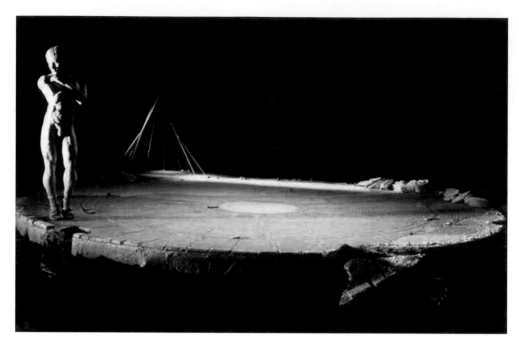

Figure 10.2 Barry Purves' *Achilles* © Barry Purves/C4/Bare Boards Productions

means. But if you use it as a mantra when going over your ideas, and planning your moves, it will help you.

None of these skills are achieved overnight – people take days over moves. A very good student I knew, doing a project she had to complete in three days, spent two days without shooting a single frame, just thinking about her character. The exercise was to complete an action in character – walking through a door, find a surprise, and react. She spent two days thinking about her puppet's character and motivation. So that when it came to the actual animation, it was carried out quickly because she knew exactly how the puppet would move: how he would put his hand on the door knob and walk though the doorway, what he would see and how he would react to it. The animation was almost automatic to her.

comedy and comic timing

In animation, as opposed to real life, you may have to exaggerate your reactions for maximum effect. It is not a simple matter of rules – but to get a feel for it you have to act it out and develop your intuition. Remember to anticipate the movement to help it read. However small the movement it is still helped by a small anticipation.

Where you can really see timing at work is in comedy. For comic timing watch the geniuses of comedy and mime at work and study their timing – how they set up a gag. Charlie Chaplin, Laurel and Hardy, Buster Keaton – they were great masters of timing. Phil Silvers as Sgt Bilko, or Tommy Cooper, Eric Morecambe of Morecambe and Wise; and Jaques Tati's Monsieur Hulot. These are all people who have learned how long to hold a silence, or when to put in a shrug, or an eye movement to convey a big moment, because their incomes depend on getting a laugh.

The cartoon 'take' is generally accepted as a 2D convention with highly dramatic squash and stretch action. Eyes popping out on stalks, tongues dropping to the floor, like Tex Avery's wolf in *Red Hot Riding Hood*. With model animation every now and then an inventive animator has ignored the static qualities of the medium and pushed it further. Richard Golezsowski, whose successful series Rex the Runt, about a group of doggy characters, employed plenty of squash and stretch, with huge, exaggerated movements by animating on glass, thereby avoiding the constrictions of gravity.

But there's no reason why you can't use some of the typical comic conventions in stop frame animation. If you are doing a 'take' as in a comic reaction, the character can anticipate, hunch their shoulders, and then turn their head toward the action. This turning of the head can be repeated two or three times for effect (see Figure 10.3). Maybe the arms will go in the opposite direction (to counter the force of the head turn). Concentrate on the body movement first and the expression at the end. This gives much more impact. If the expression changes along with the speed of the move it kills the anticipation.

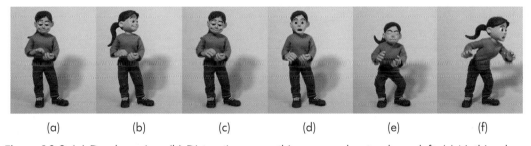

| (a) | (b) | (c) | (d) | (e) | (f) |

Figure 10.3 (a) Daydreaming. (b) Distraction: something causes her to glance left. (c) Nothing has registered, she has returned to her original pose. (d) Realization. The jaw drops and eyes widen. (e) Anticipation, the girl hunches down, so the next move will have more impact. Note the ponytail is following the movement down. (f) Action and reaction! The arms swing in the opposite direction to the head, to counter the weight shift. Courtesy ScaryCat Studio

The expression on the face should only change at the end of the move. There are various ways to do this comedy take – it can be extended with a small anticipation before Figure 10.3(d). If you try this sequence, play around with the timings till you've caught the transition from daydreaming to shock.

Comedy run: this is such a cliché, but good fun to try it, as once again it's a 2D convention, but can be done with our puppet – *big* anticipation pose, and then take puppet away, leave the stage empty! There are different ways to create a blur left by the character. Have the puppet attached to wire so that she can be swung across the set as you expose the frame, or as Pete Lord suggests, create a blur of Plasticine. Of course it can always be done in post production! You won't learn anything about animation from post production, but you will learn a lot from trying different timings, angles and keeping your puppet balanced.

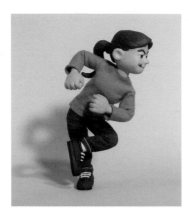

Figure 10.4 Puppet pose in typical comedy run anticipation. Courtesy ScaryCat Studio

This brings us back to persistence of vision. So how much does the audience need to see? One of the great things about the human mind is that it fills in the blanks. That is how film works after all, we actually spend an awful lot of the time looking at a black screen, but we don't notice that. It's something to consider when planning your moves in animation. You can do the same sort of thing with kicking a football. To get the right impact with a foot kicking a ball is a tricky combination, as it relies on speed (and all the complexities of Newton's laws of motion!) – difficult to achieve with model animation. But what do you, the audience, need to see to understand that a great moment in sporting history has just occurred? You need to see the footballer approach the ball, draw his foot back – and – *wham!* The ball going into the net! Perhaps you don't need to see the actual kick and the trajectory of the ball for you to believe that that footballer scored that goal. Knowing what to leave out comes with experience.

eyelines

To convince your audience that your character is alive it is important to get the eyelines right. Think about the focus of their vision; whether they are gazing into the distance or at something close-up, the focus will change. If it's very close the pupils will be slightly crossed.

blinking

How often to blink? Well – don't go mad – but it's quite a good idea to blink on a head move. If the character's startled and does a 'take' they might do a blink as the head draws back. People blink a lot when they talk. A shyer character will blink more than a bold one. The actor Michael Caine, when playing a difficult character, has learned to keep blinking to a minimum.

Have plenty of flesh-tone clay to cover the eyes standing by as eyelids just disappear. A one-frame blink, with the eye covered works fine, but you might want to refine that by giving it three frames.

With repeat movements, like blinking with the eyelid going down and up, you have to realize how it would read to the audience. Putting the eyelids half way both on the lids down frame and the lids up frame will make that position more dominant than the open or shut frame, as you are seeing it twice, so the shut frame won't register – the lids will only seem to go half way down.

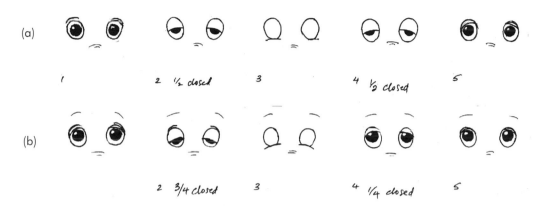

Figure 10.5 (a) Blink (single frame). This sequence results in the impression of $\frac{1}{2}$ closed eyes, as frame 3 does not register. (b) Effective blink sequence

more than one character

If you are dealing with more than one character, you have to think about which one is drawing the audience's eye. And where do you want the audience to look? Obviously the soundtrack helps, but it's a good idea to always think in terms of mime, so that you draw the eye towards the right character. Block out your moves so that you know they will maintain the right composition for your intentions, that one character isn't masking the other, or up-staging the other and so on. Make sure the camera is focussed on the right character at the right time.

Keeping the secondary character out of the limelight is an important dramatic technique. Watch how still secondary characters stay when the hero is taking centre stage. Unnecessary movement distracts the eye of the viewer. As we are not dealing with live actors we have to make sure our characters stay 'alive', in other words that they don't just 'freeze'. An occasional blink or a very small shift of weight is enough to keep a character alive.

subtle character animation

Thinking always in terms of comedy effects can lead to the animation losing its flavour and becoming repetitious, going from pose to pose: Hold – move, hold – move, hold.

Subtlety is created by taking the animation further, using observation – looking for the expressions people use that are most telling of their character.

> *We did some live reference work for* Chicken Run *for ease of communication – so that Nick could get the ideas across. You could pick up what he was interested in right away – an eye movement – timing of a head gesture. ... Generally you wouldn't follow the whole thing – but key things – and have them on hand.*
> Jeff Newitt, animated Mr and Mrs Tweedy on *Chicken Run*

In his short film *Canhead*, the American animator Tim Hittle animates the hero, Jay Clay, casting aside his weapon in a little, but beautifully timed movement that shows a huge, complicated emotion. In this movement he conveys disgust at the appearance of his own aggressive nature and an ability to shrug it off as quickly as it appeared.

> *In my own films there is no dialogue. The characters are just made from clay so I am able to sculpt any expressions that I need. A lot can be done with an eyebrow shifting or a mouth turning up or down. I watch silent films, athletes, and people in general. My main source of reference is myself. I go through the actions over and over with a stopwatch until I am sure of the timing, and then it is a matter of execution.*

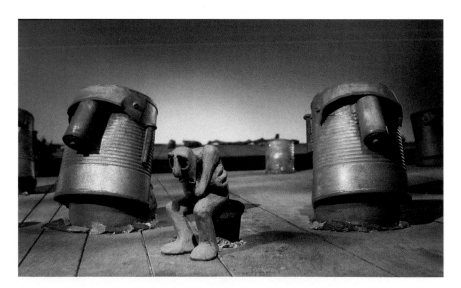

Figure 10.6 Still from *Canhead*. © Timothy Hittle

Look at how much of your character needs to move. In *Creature Comforts* Nick Park animated the Brazilian jaguar to start with, swishing its tail back and forth as he spoke. But very quickly he realized it was a distraction and just left it to hang. Only move what's necessary. In so much animation, especially early computer animation, there is too much movement.

To make another comparison, using Aardman's skills as an example again, the penguin, Feathers McGraw, in *The Wrong Trousers* is a magnificent example of under acting. Guionne Leroy, a Belgian animator who worked on *Toy Story*, *Nightmare Before Christmas* and *Chicken Run* elaborates: 'With the penguin in Wrong Trousers, Steve (Box) was really teasing us, making the penguin stop – the sense of surprise. He can make a character move in a way that's full of life inside.'

So pacing and rhythm is enhanced by putting some stillness into your acting – only move what needs to move, or what helps the story along. Think yourself into the character and let your instinct guide you.

If your character is to be still – you want them to have reached a comfortable position to hold as a still pose. If they haven't achieved that 'relaxed' look – a hold isn't going to work.

Creating subtle animation is a subjective business – research, sifting through reference material and constant observation is needed. Practising observation through sketching and life drawing, study of acting – using all these different approaches can only develop your skill, and then it can translate into whichever medium you want to apply it to – it is the essence of animation.

All animators put something of themselves into their puppets. It is a very full emotional experience for the model animator, as the performance is a one-off, just like a stage performance.

> *You feel this incredible connection, you feel you're giving them your soul, you're giving them your life, giving them your emotions. You're being a kind of channel for them really, allowing them to really become alive, allowing them to live with all the juice that they have. It's a wonderful, beautiful work. If you have this desire to offer your hands, your body and your sensibility at the service of expressing a life that is contained within a puppet, but needs a conscience to bloom – that's the beauty of it. To me that's the essence of animation.*
>
> Guionne Leroy

chapter 11

filming

Stopmo can be nerve racking. You start at one end and work through to the other. Any sour frame along the way can contaminate the whole shot. It is much like a live performance and each shot is unique, if you have to do it twice it may be better or worse but it can never be the same. You have to stay awake and aware of lights blowing or props moving or the camera getting bumped. You learn to know the correct sound of the camera advancing the film one frame at a time. If the shot comes back with problems it can be a heartbreaker. You are always taking a chance to be disappointed. But when it comes back and you've nailed it and everything you wanted is there, it is a joy! That's when I begin to feel like an artist.

Tim Hittle

You have far more control making an animated film than any other kind – you control the weather, the lighting conditions and the timing, all the elements that shorten the life of 'live' film directors. Now it's no longer planning, but the real thing – and you really don't get a second chance – so approach everything with patience, a cool head – and get into the animation.

Once you have your script, storyboard, sets built, models made, sound breakdown and animation instructions on your bar chart or X-sheet, you are ready to shoot.

filming information

If you are shooting on film, you need to choose your film stock. There is a huge choice of film stocks, mainly designed for live filming. You can get very good advice from film laboratories (see appendix 1) as to which stock would suit your conditions, but generally you would be shooting on colour negative film, either a 50ft roll of Super 8, or a 100ft roll of 16mm. Once exposed the film is sent to the labs, who will develop it then telecine it on to the format you want, Beta SP, DV or VHS, so that you can edit on your computer.

shutter speed

This is the length of time the film in your camera is exposed to the light coming through the lens. In animation, rather than 'live' filming, as there is no continuous action, the shutter speed can be very slow, anything from a quarter of a second to 6 seconds. This then relates to the amount of lighting you use for your set and accordingly how large or small the lens aperture or f-stop is set at.

f-stops

The lens aperture on the camera is a diaphragm that operates like the iris of an eye, closing down to shut out light, or opening up to let more in. On a manual camera it is controlled by turning part of the lens barrel. The size of the aperture is measured in f-stops. The f-stop numbers are an agreed sequence relating to the brightness of the image: each change to a higher number halves the amount of light passing through your lens. The numbers typically start at f/2; f/2.8; f/4; f/5.6; f/8; f/11; and f/16, with f/2 being wide open, letting a lot of light in, and f/16 being a smaller hole, letting less light through.

light meter

Once you've set up your ASA or film speed and shutter speed on the meter, you will want to measure the 'incident' light that falls on your puppet, or your background. The white dome that comes with your meter measures the light falling on the object. Place the dome as close as possible to the object you are filming and angle the dome to the camera, so that the incident light, falling on your puppet, is the same as the light falling on your meter. That will give you your light reading, the f-stop.

depth of field

Your depth of field means the area of your shot that is in focus. In animation, because you are working on a small scale, very much closer to the action than you would be when making a 'live' film, your depth of field is much more critical. Closing down your lens aperture, or using a wide-angle lens can increase the depth of field. The smaller your aperture, the more light you will need (see Figure 11.1).

colour temperature

Colour temperature is measured in degrees Kelvin. The scale of colour temperature ranges roughly from red through to blue, the brighter the light, the hotter or bluer it becomes, so that light measured at dawn or sunset is red(ish) and light measured at noon is blue(ish). The typical colour temperature given for daylight is measured as the sun at midday, a blue light: 5500°Kelvin or K. Domestic tungsten light measures 3200K.

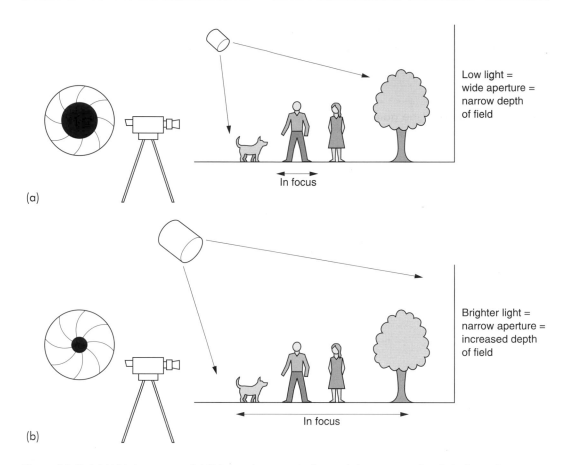

Figure 11.1 (a) With less powerful lighting the area in front of the camera that is in focus is reduced. (b) With more light, the camera's iris can be smaller, increasing the depth of field and helping to overcome the sense of a 'miniature' world

Colour correction gels can be bought from lighting supply companies or photographic retailers so that you can create your lighting effects. Be aware that any filters that go in front of your light source or your lens will *reduce* the light and affect the f-stop.

You can buy film that is balanced for daylight or tungsten light. As you are working indoors, you would use film that is balanced for tungsten light. The first thing you record on your film reel should be a colour chart or grey scale, available from your film stock supplier, for the film laboratories to have as reference and they will set their telecine accordingly. It should be shot under a white unfiltered light from the camera position.

light-proofing your camera

You must be sure that your camera is absolutely light tight. It's worth testing with some left over footage if you have some: leave it in the camera for a few hours in a lit room, then send for processing. Even if it doesn't seem to have a light leak, it may be worth taping up the doors with black tape, or putting a black cloth over the camera to be sure.

loading film into your camera

Always load 'daylight' spools in subdued light. First remove the take-up spool and clean out the camera, checking the gate for 'hairs' or accumulated emulsion that can cause scratching. Load in your new film and run it through the gate, then put in the take-up spool and make sure the film is taking up on it properly. Then shut the camera and run on for 5 ft to clear any fogged film. Put some tape over your camera to show that it is loaded.

When you open up the side of your camera to remove the exposed film, always have the empty can waiting. Then tape up the exposed can of film and label it with the following:

- to: name of film labs
- name of production
- film type
- date exposed.

You can get black light-tight 'changing bags' from photographic suppliers for loading film. It takes a bit of practice, but it's essential if you are loading 400ft rolls for which you would use a separate film magazine.

shooting with video

It's amazing how much animation is still shot on film. It seems to go with the sensibilities of the animator, having a more hands-on approach. Now though, using frame grabber systems, there is very little reason not to shoot on video, especially if your budget is small. And a digital movie camera is going to give you a great picture with all the ease of having your images fed straight into your computer.

However, if you are shooting with a cheaper video camera, there are a couple of things to note.

white balance for video

You need to tell the video camera what 'white' is by showing it something white under your lighting conditions. Most cameras will have automatic white balancing, but for older cameras, you'll need to do it manually. Set up a white card in your key light, point the camera at it so that most of the viewfinder is filled with white and go through the white balance procedure for your camera. Do the white balance before you put any filters on, then the filters will do their job. If you white balance afterwards, the camera will try to normalize everything.

If you can't have manual over-ride on your video camera, **remember to let the automatic controls settle before you take the shot**. This is especially important to remember when you're wearing black. Many animators wear dark clothing so as not to reflect light on to the set. If you're wearing black and lean in to move your puppet, then lean out and take a frame before the exposure has settled, the frame will be burnt out.

camera moves

Consider carefully the need for a camera move, as it is a very time-consuming business in the planning and is very hard to control. It can only really be achieved successfully at a price.

- **Pan:** Moving the camera from side to side on a fixed tripod. Take into account the focus difference from one side of the set to the middle of your set, and check for lens flare from beginning to end.
- **Tilt:** Moving the camera up and down on a fixed tripod. Once again, focusses may change so remember to check.
- **Track:** Moving the camera forwards, backwards or side to side, best done on some sort of track. Professionally done with computerized motion control on a track.
- **Zoom:** Zooming in with a lens is tricky as, depending on the quality of your lens, it can create a telescoping effect with your background. It's not recommended to use a zoom too much, but if you must, it may well be safer than attempting to track in.

All camera moves should be planned in advance. You need at least a good solid tripod with a pan and tilt head, or better still a tracking system. It is possible to slide cameras along on table tops, and correct the position on the screen, or use a mic boom to swing a camera over a set but this is very difficult to control and is not going to look that great! However, you can add batons as guides on the table top to give you a fixed track and place your camera on a roller skate base for a doll, and this will improve your chances. Make sure you have checked the focus for the length of your move and marked up the different focus positions on white **camera tape** around the lens barrel.

There are many ways of marking off your increments for the move, as long as your pointer, either on the camera or geared head, is rigid and comes close enough to your markings for accuracy. Martin Shann, Aardman Animations, remembers marking up knicker elastic with calibrations for camera moves: 'You could use the same piece and then stretch it for different distances!'

panning or tracking speeds

If you are planning your move to follow a character walking across the screen, you should plan your move in accordance with the timing of the animation. The camera move will need to increase its speed from zero at the start of the move and slow down again at the end of the move. If your pan starts too soon, it looks as though you are anticipating the puppet's move. You probably want to literally 'follow' the puppet, so make your pan slightly behind the puppet's move.

motion control

A professional animation studio would generally approach a camera move nowadays with computerized motion control. A motion control rig is a huge robotic 'arm' with a rotating head that can move the camera into almost any position you need it. The camera operator programmes the rig depending on the shot required. This data then enables the rig to be used again, creating exactly the same movement which, in turn, allows for several passes each matching exactly the ones preceding it. This process allows for multiple exposures of the film with perfect film registration. This programmed data, used within the original shoot, of either a model environment or live-action background, may then also be transferred to a computer in order to 'drive' the camera within a computer animated sequence. Alternatively one may choose to use chroma key – 'green-screen' techniques to shoot the background separately from the foreground, or the animation elements. To achieve perfect synchronization of separate moving elements is a specialized process known as match moving.

lighting

What is your light source? If your action is indoors, your light source can be from interior light or from daylight coming in through the windows. If your location is outdoors, the sun or the moon would be your main source of light.

In a traditional lighting set-up you would have a **'key'** light, a **'fill'** light and a **'back'** light The key light is the main source of light representing the sun, so set your strongest light at the position of your 'sun' or 'moon'. The fill light helps to soften the shadows cast by the key light, and the back light or **'rim'** light shining from above and behind your character helps to highlight them, and separate them from the background.

Film and video don't register light and shade in the same way as our eyes do, so we find things look better if the shadows are reduced. In order to reduce the shadows, we use fill lights, which are diffused or 'bounced'. You can turn a light to bounce off a white surface; a polystyrene (Styrofoam) board is often used, this creates a very soft, even light with almost no shadow. The very simplest effective lighting can be achieved using just one light. Use this as your 'key' and place a sheet of polystyrene (Styrofoam) so that it picks up the light spilling off the set and 'bounces it back onto your subject, lightening the black shadow caused by the key. This, after all, is what happens with natural sun light. See Figure 11.2.

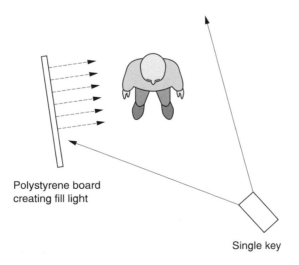

Polystyrene board
creating fill light

Single key

Figure 11.2 Achieving lighting with fill using only one (key) light source and polystyrene (styrofoam) board

You can cover lights with a variety of diffusion filters, and you can use gobos (see chapter 4) to create atmospheric shadows. If you need to cut down and soften the light a bit, you can put an old metal sieve directly in front of your lamp.

Multiple shadows can create confusion, so try to keep one main light source or direction.

For moonlight, use back-lighting to cast an edge of light on characters, hedges etc. Moonlight is a hard light, like the sun, but less. You can use a blue gel (if you must); it does help us believe it's moonlight – and use some bounce off the back-lights to fill the front of the set.

A lot of series animation is shot with a very uniform-looking bright but diffuse light. This is a safe way of creating 'shadowless' lighting, with all the lights bounced off white or shining through a large screen of diffusion material known as 'trace' (looks like stiff tracing paper). This can make the characters look a little flat and their environment highly unrealistic, which may be the desired effect.

The lights need to complement each other in terms of output. You would want your fill light to give you about a maximum of two f-stops less than your key light. Similarly if you have an exterior that's seen from a room window, that will be a brighter light than the interior, maybe one stop more than the (interior) key light.

lighting the background

Halogen 'garage' lamps throw a good spread of light. The sky is brightest at the horizon, at sunset, sunrise and at noon. So it is best lit from below, with the light falling off towards the top. Your light meter should read about a stop more than the key light. Avoid any 'hot' spots (unless you want to create one for a sunrise or sunset). Garage lights may need a bit of diffusion as they can throw a 'streaky' light.

As with anything, the more you can spend, the better your lighting will be. There are lights designed for every purpose and every situation, but I have seen great atmospheric lighting (albeit with a shallow depth of field) created by two desk lamps artfully placed.

To avoid lens flare, check that no light, especially the back lighting, is shining directly into the lens. If it is, it could ruin the shot so you need to protect the lens by flagging it. The lens hood may be enough, but if not you could attach a purpose-made black 'flag', or use black wrap (heavy duty foil) that you can shape.

health and safety issues

Using lighting and electrical equipment is always potentially hazardous. Overloading any system could blow fuses, if not your equipment. Take sensible precautions for yourself and anyone working with you to protect yourselves and your equipment. Some safety tips for setting up lighting include:

1. Check that you have enough power to cope with the lighting you are setting up. A 13-amp circuit is standard for the UK, 15 amps for the US. No single normal circuit can supply more than 3100 watts (UK) or 1800 watts of power (US).
2. So first check the **amperage** (amp rating) of the electrical circuit you are using, and then the total **wattage** of the lamps *and equipment* you are using. If the total is above the wattage mentioned, you will need outlets from two different circuits, which could mean running a lead from another part of the building.
3. The UK standard voltage is 240 volts, in the US it is 100–120 V. The sum you need to remember is: watts = volts × amps. Use extension cables that are powerful enough to deal with the current you are running through them. A cable drum usually has this information on it (i.e. max 7 amps wound/13 amps unwound).
4. Using an extension cable on a drum for lighting is not recommended, but if you have to, completely unwind the cable, as the heat generated could easily overheat and ignite the cable. Make sure the cable is capable of taking the power you want through it.
5. Cables shouldn't be frayed, and once the lighting position has been set, cables should be made as unobtrusive as possible, with all cables on the floor taped down with 'gaffer' or 'duct' tape and hanging loops of cable should be clipped out of the way. In other words, ensure that no-one can trip over a cable, or knock against a lamp stand. Use hazard warning tape – the kind building sites use to warn pedestrians – to alert people to danger areas on your set.
6. When changing bulbs, first ensure the lamp is cool enough to touch, and, second, don't handle the bulbs with bare skin as the sweat from your fingers will shorten the life of the bulb – fit it using the plastic wrapping it comes with. The colour temperature of a new bulb will be different from the old one. As a bulb ages the light coming from it becomes warmer (nearer the red end of the spectrum) and the new bulb will be brighter. You might want to correct the colour a little with a gel to match it up to the rest of the shot.

your own welfare

When you set up your shot, try to leave yourself some room to manoeuvre. This can get difficult with the accumulation of lights, set and various stands holding bits and pieces. You've got a long time to spend with that set and the repetitious moves you make when you're involved with the animation can make you very uncomfortable. One tip is to put your animation control unit or keypad in a different position each day, so that you vary your movements. It sounds a bit precious, but could save a very stiff neck.

If you are working in a cold studio on a concrete floor, you will spend so much time on your feet, it's worth putting a thick piece of polystyrene on the floor to stand on where you are animating. It helps keep you warm and helps to ease leg ache.

special effects – tips and hints

With stop frame filming the most ordinary occurrence becomes an extraordinary challenge and calls for an inventive solution. As stop frame has developed over the years in little studios, separated from each other by hundreds and thousands of miles, there has been very little communication – nobody wrote a book of rules. Each studio had its own way of dealing with water, fire and smoke effects. And the good news is that communication hasn't changed this – there are still a hundred and one different ways of achieving these effects, and everyone has a different answer. There are no definitive rules.

double exposure and matting

When using film cameras some effects are created 'in camera', e.g. double exposure and matting. But so much is now achievable with effects in post production that some of the classic methods could soon be forgotten.

A matte is a very thin shaped black metal or plastic device that can slot in front of the camera's gate allowing part of your image to be masked, preventing the film being exposed in the masked area. You then cover the lens with the lens cap in order to wind the film back to the exact frame at the beginning of the shot, and matte the exposed part of the frame and film your other shot. The matte shape would have to be cut to whatever purpose you need.

A more sophisticated form of matting is called 'checkerboarding' (frontlight/back light), a technique used by Ray Harryhausen. You shoot one frame of the character lit normally from the front, followed by a frame where the character is silhouetted by an illuminated background. This creates a perfect matte of your character, who can then be superimposed onto a background.

With a camera you can wind back you can also create a double-exposure. If you want to create a neon glow, the neon effect is created by making a first filmed 'pass' with only the neon signs lit up and everything else blacked out. Then the film is wound back (lens capped up) to the start, everything on the set is properly lit, including the neon signs, and the second pass is made. It is important to compensate with your exposure for the fact that you are exposing the film twice, however low the lighting in the first pass. If you are doing several passes to allow for separate animation elements, it can be very easy to overexpose film, so careful calculation of exposures must be taken.

using glass

A large pane of glass placed in front of the background allows all sorts of special effects to be created. You can animate water droplets running down, splashes, smoke, explosions. It also enables animation to go ahead in a sort of 2D/3D, allowing more squash and stretch and dynamic movement of all sorts without the need for rigging, as in Richard Goleszowski's series *Rex the Runt*. Of course the animation doesn't have to stay on the one plane, the background can be animated as well. Lighting becomes much trickier as you may be casting shadows onto your background. You may also want to give some dimension to your characters – so side/top lighting at about 45° to the camera helps.

Reflections in the glass have to be cancelled out, by blacking out the camera with black card on a frame covering everything but the lens. A **polarizing** filter will help reduce or eliminate reflections. If you are using more than one pane of glass, or if you have glass that is too thick, it could become a problem that there will be some light loss through the glass – it also has a greenish colour which you might need to take into account. Optically correct glass, with no green in, is expensive, and you can also get filters for the camera which counteract

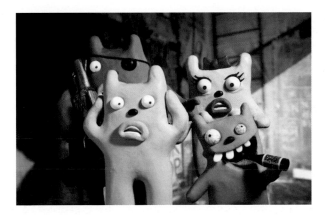

Figure 11.3 *Rex the Runt*, created by Richard Goleszowski. © Aardman/Rex the Runt/BBC Worldwide Ltd 1991

the green. But generally speaking it's only worth being aware of, in case you start to get problems.

chroma key or green screen/blue screen

Shooting your characters on a plain blue or green background (chroma key) is commonly used nowadays as a method of putting your characters into a situation that is either too expensive or difficult to create as a set. Then the two images are put together digitally in post production.

To set up a blue/green screen, you need a large fluorescent colour area, preferably blue or green, if necessary covering the floor as well as the background. This should be lit overall, separately from the lighting for your characters and objects. When lighting your characters/objects you want to light them in a way that will complement the background you are putting them into, at the same time creating as little shadow as possible. You will need to shoot the animation at the same camera angle as the shot they are going to be matched into.

fire

Again, there are many solutions, depending on the size of flame you want – people will matte filmed fire but one can create more controlled effects using reflective material like Scotchlite®. It's used for road signs and when light shines directly on to it, can be almost blindingly bright. This makes it useful for effects such as a striking match, or bright flames. As it is a sticky-backed plastic material, it can be cut out into the shapes you want. Shine a small spotlight on it directly from the camera, and alternate shapes.

explosions

Depending on the style of your film, try cartoon explosions. Replace the puppet with cut-out card explosion shapes changing shape and colour every 4 frames as in Peter Peake's spoof children's short *Pib and Pog*. Explosions can be created very simply with paint on glass

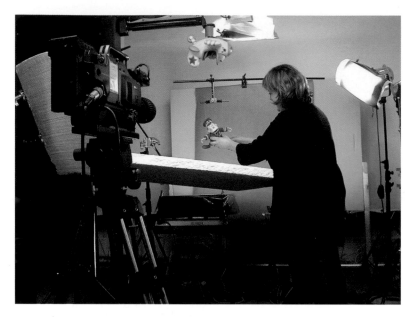

Figure 11.4 Shooting a scene from Cosgrove Hall Film's *Engie Benjy* against blue screen

placed between the camera and set. Front lit Scotchlite, as suggested in 'fire', can also be used for explosion effects.

camera shake

Explosions, earthquakes and volcanoes can all be accompanied by camera shake to enhance any effect. A few frames right and left of the original position, and maybe up and down too.

rain

Make a first pass filming rain (a situation that has to be very carefully monitored as you have water and electricity closely combined) against a black background. Back light the rain to make it show up. For the rain, if you use a hose, you will need a large area so that you can get well back to allow an even fall of drops. It helps if the size of your shot and the size of rain drops are compatible with the size of your matching shot. You could always give yourself a range of 'stock' shots in different scales while you're at it.

snow

Make a first pass using polystyrene beads or shredded paper against a black background, this time lit from the front. Again remember to make the size of shot compatible.

footprints in the snow

I found a posting on Anthony Scott's website, **Stopmotionanimation.com**, asking how somebody would make footprints in the snow. After various complex theories had been put forward, Anthony himself answered, as he had animated Jack Skellington walking through snow in *Nightmare Before Christmas*:

> I animated shots with snow in the 'Poor Jack' sequence. The snow was made of Styrofoam that was sculpted and attached to the wooden set. To create footprints, I just punched thru the Styrofoam and drilled a hole to tie down Jack's foot. It was a simple process although I had to be careful not to crush the snow as I climbed onto the set. I made a special wooden platform that I placed over the snow for certain shots just so I could reach the puppet without crushing the foam.
>
> I can't remember exactly what I used to punch through . . . probably a wooden tool of some kind. I did use a framegrabber but I also gauged the puppet so that I could keep track of all the pieces of torn cloth as well as its legs.

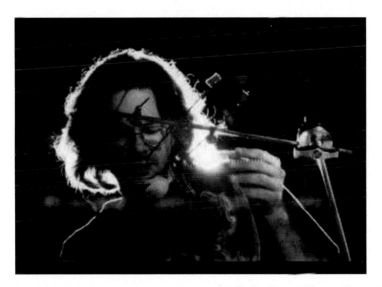

Figure 11.5 Anthony Scott animating Jack Skellington in Tim Burton's *Nightmare Before Christmas*. The scene has Jack's clothing in tatters and Anthony used gauges to keep track of the position of each fluttering piece of cloth as he animated. Photo © Jim Mattlosz

American animators tend to use gauges far more than UK animators, it's just a different way of working that has grown up between the two countries.

water

Add either splashes cast out of clear resin or cut out of clear or frosted acetate, randomly appearing for two/four frames here and there. Glycerine is thick enough to use for drips running down a window. Use KY Jelly on a reflective surface to animate ripples on a pond. For pouring water, or a torrent, use cling wrap or cellophane.

smoke

Cotton wool teased out to thin wisps.

fog/mist

A few layers of net stretched on a frame catching the light and animating gently could create fog. Tristan Oliver, DOP on Aardman's *The Wrong Trousers*, lit stretches of net further back in the set for shafts of sunlight on an early morning street scene; this helped to create a sense of depth in the scene.

wind

This is a bit fiddly to achieve on a whole set if it's an exterior, although it would bring a lot of life to the usual stiff trees and hedges. It would mean having all your branches made with aluminium wire that you could animate. To achieve an effect of wind with curtains, thread thin aluminium wire into thin seams on the fabric, so that it can be animated. Flags can be treated similarly. Alternatively, the fabric could be glued to heavy duty foil.

Leaves tumbling by could be animated on glass over the set.

motion blur

To achieve an illusion of speed, you could either move your background from side to side while exposing (not always an easy option!). An exposure of between ½ to 2 seconds helps here. This would give you a blurred background. Or you could attach your character to the camera on a rig so that it was locked into the camera move, and shoot on the move, again with a long shutter speed. This technique was used for the motorbike sequence in Aardman's *A Close Shave* and the train sequence in *The Wrong Trousers*.

consider the editor

While filming, if your budget can stand it, consider the editor. They can always use a little extra at the beginning and end of each shot so that they can get the cut in exactly the right place for the rhythm and pace of the piece. If you are walking a puppet on, start it right off screen. As well as helping you to get into the rhythm with your animation, it also allows a shadow to precede the puppet if the angles of the lighting cause it. Let your opening move start a little earlier than you'd planned, and the same with the final move.

final checks before you hit that button

Is everything there that you need? Or is there something there that you don't want?

- **Do you have spare everything?** You don't want to get started and then have to break off in search of bits and pieces. It's very important to keep your rhythm and concentration going. Do you have spare bits of Plasticine/clay in the right colour for eyelids, teeth, spare hands standing by?
- **Are your sculpting tools all there?** Small mirror to check lip sync; lanolin – free wet wipes to keep hands clean?

- Check that **nothing is on the set that shouldn't be there**. Check around the four corners of the frame: that will remind you of your composition, as well as show up anything that shouldn't be there.
- If you're shooting on film, is the camera loaded? A loaded camera should have tape around it or its film magazine, describing the film stock, date it's loaded (and in a studio, the loader's name so they know who to blame!). If you're not confident the camera is absolutely light tight: does it have a black cloth/black tape over it?
- Is the lens in **focus**? Is the **aperture** correct? Shutter speed?
- Make sure the lens cap is off, I know it's obvious, but ...
- Has the film been run on? You need to run on about a foot of film once you've loaded, so you won't be shooting on exposed film.
- Is the camera **locked off**/tripod weighted/glued to the floor?
- Check for any unwanted **reflections and shadows** – there may be reflections in shiny areas that you don't see looking at the set, but you can see through the viewfinder. You can buy dulling spray from photographic shops, but check later in the shot that it hasn't smudged.
- **Mark it:** identify the shot with a board giving the title of the film, scene number, and 'take' number if necessary. This is helpful to the editor identifying your shots. If you have forgotten to put it on the start of the shot, it can go on the end, but it must be **upside down**.

sending your film to the labs

When you have taken the film out of the camera, and it has been canned up in a light-proof black bag inside a tin that is then carefully taped up, label the can clearly with the title of the film, the film stock, the date exposed and your company name. Put the name of the lab it's going to. Along with it should go a camera report sheet describing the conditions and details of the filming. The lab can provide a book of these sheets for you.

glossary

black wrap: a heavy duty black aluminium foil. Many uses, including quick fix flagging of the lens hood, or making mini flags for the set. Available from film and lighting suppliers.

camera tape: generally white or yellow – a strong tape for a variety of uses. Traditionally used for taping up a can of film to go to the labs. Useful for putting down marks as one can mark increments on it with a fine pen. Available from film and lighting suppliers.

fill light: light used to fill strong black shadows created by the key light. Can be reflected light rather than a lamp itself.

flag: a shaped flat black metal rectangle, can be bought in different sizes, used to cut or control where light falls. 'Flagging' the light simply means blocking it in some way. Large flags are available as black fireproofed material over a rectangular frame. A 'flag' arm can be a small articulated arm attached to a camera mounting, to block lens flare, or a much larger articulated arm used for bigger lamps at a distance.

incident light: the light that falls on a subject.

key light: The main, strongest lamp: either replicating the sun or the moon, or the main source of lighting in an interior.

matte: a mask, blacking off part of the image so that it will not be exposed, placed either in the camera between lens and gate or just on glass in front of lens, allowing two images (or more) to be superimposed.

reflected light: the light reflected off a subject.

rim light: lamp used to backlight characters, giving separation from the background. Also helps to 'glamorize' a character by adding a glow at the back of the head.

Scotchlite: made by 3M. Available from lighting/photographic distributors: sticky backed plastic with a coating of minute glass beads. Used for reflective road signs, etc.

spot meter: a more specialized light meter used for measuring small areas of reflected light, or measuring a distant object. The spot meter should be used standing at the camera position.

chapter 12

post production

chapter	• *timecode*
summary	• *sound*

Rushes are the most terrifying thing on God's earth – exciting but so raw. There are no sound effects. And you have to explain to some executive producer, 'there will be sound here' and you feel you have to explain your way all through the rushes. It's so painful watching it. But the joy of making something move – then you watch it on film and it's not yours anymore. You still have the muscle memory – you can remember what was going on in the world when you were shooting it and you can feel your bones aching when you see a particular scene. But you can't do anything about it – it's gone!

Barry Purves

Barry describes the moment that you sit down with an executive producer and look through the film that has just returned from the labs, without sound, with every mistake that has happened on full view to everybody. It is a more visceral experience than tape rushes, which you can see as you go along. With film, the magic comes out of the black box, and there is the tension of checking the lab report before even looking at the film rushes – where every exposure mistake, scratch or (even worse) film fogging, is identified and charted for you by the lab technician.

'Rushes' or 'dailies' is the term for an ungraded or 'rushed' print of your film. This is becoming a rarer process now, as your negative is usually digitized by the labs or by the post-production house in the order of assemblage you require, so that you can work on it without touching film. It is cheaper to ask the labs simply to process your negative and have it forwarded to the post-production house for digitization.

Alternatively if you are working on computer, once the animation sequences are completed, replace your animatic on the computer with each sequence and trim the shots as necessary.

timecode

Once you start putting sound and image together you need to ensure that you have time-code to match or sync sound and image together.

Until the advent of video recording, sound to film synchronization was carried out mechanically. This mainly relied on sprockets in the film and sprocketed recording tape. Relative timing adjustments could be made by slipping sprocket holes. The same sprocket holes were used to maintain synchronization. Video tape hasn't got any sprocket holes, so when video arrived an electronic equivalent was needed to take the place of mechanical methods of synchronization. This method is called timecode, and you need to set your timecode at the frame-rate selected by the Society of Motion Picture and Television Engineers (SMPTE) depending on which part of the world you are working in. The EBU (European Broadcasting Union) standard of 25 fps is used throughout Europe, Australia and wherever the mains frequency is 50 Hz and the colour TV system is PAL or SECAM. For America this is 30 fps based on the mains frequency of 60 Hz (the TV system is NTSC). The remaining rate of 24 fps is required for film work and is rarely used for audio.

If you have been working with a small budget, you will have edited the film as much as possible in advance with the storyboard, and only need to edit the film in terms of a few frames cut out here and there. However, if you have had a bit more spare time and money you will have given the shots a little overlap at the start and finish, to allow the editor a bit more leeway with their cuts. This will help them achieve smoother edits, when they are cutting on a move.

But there is still the possibility that the film needs cutting more seriously...

> When I first worked at Aardman I was working with Dave Sproxton a lot. And that was quite an education because he's not an animator, although he knows it all inside out, how it goes together, the performance etc. But to cut stuff with him – he's just not precious about the animation. And you learn so much from somebody like that. He'll say 'well that doesn't work, let's lop it off!' and you think 'My God! My work!...' So you have to get that out the way and then you're not so precious about all those beautiful little bits. They aren't the whole, they may help the story, but they aren't the story...
>
> Jeff Newitt

You will then need to make up an edit decision list (EDL) where all the cuts, mixes, fades in or out relate to the timecoded numbers on the film, which is then sent to the post-production editor. The post-production editor will digitally clean up the film, wiping any rigs, correcting any set shift, correcting colour and hue, brightness and contrasts. This process can get expensive and it's important to make a decision in advance of how far you are prepared to go with post production – as any amount of correction seems possible at this stage, but always at a cost. It's far better to have avoided those situations by planning well, only using rigs when absolutely necessary and being careful throughout the process.

Colour-grading, which used to be a process where the printer at the labs would take time to match the colours scene by scene, is now done digitally more often than not in the post-production house.

sound

When your edit is complete – it's time for the soundtrack, this is where sound design really matters.

Music, the characters' voices, and the layers of sound enhance the mood of the film. You have to build the soundtrack up from nothing – whether it's an interior or an exterior scene, you will need all the atmosphere sounds that make up that scene.

Interiors may have less layers of sound, but it may be important to hear the atmosphere outside – birdsong, traffic, etc. An interior will have a slight echo, as the soundwaves reverberate off the walls.

Exterior sounds have no echo – unless you are in a mountain range, or a tunnel. But they do have texture: wind; leaves rustling; water; birdsong; outer space (sound?); rain; traffic (when I worked in the BBC long ago as an assistant editor, there was a tape we always used for general traffic sounds called 'Stoke Poges'. The original recording was made standing on a roundabout in Stoke Poges – probably back in the 1960s!).

James Mather who has done sound post production for many companies including Aardman Animations explains:

> *Once the film is delivered, you get given a day a minute to track lay. For a 3 minute film you get 2–3 hours recording Foley and spot effects to picture. The Foleys are the most important stage – it's the bond between the sound effects, the music and the action. It's what makes the characters real. It's quite an art, because you don't necessarily want to create naturalistic sounds, you have to create a world that goes with these strange characters - so you have to look at them and think – is it a rubbery sound? Is it a wooden sound? And then come up with the effect that works.*

Foley artists work to the film and create effects such as footsteps, wings flapping, knuckles cracking, pencils scribbling, sounds that need to be matched in time to an action on the film. The sound editor treats the sounds, so that they sound right for the film using different recording techniques.

There are large libraries of effects disks, quite expensive to collect, but you will be much better off creating your own sounds. There are difficult sounds to create such as sirens or particular ring tones, but generally you can find the right location for your soundtrack – factory, school, café – and record a background sound of your own.

Libraries also have copyright-free music you can use, if it is the right music that's fine, but the choice of music is very important, it can really lift a film. You have to be very careful about copyright. You cannot use a music track without the permission of its author – a complex, slow and sometimes extremely expensive procedure. Even 'Happy Birthday to You' is subject to copyright laws. These laws are enforceable as soon as your film is shown to a fee-paying audience. You may only think you're going to show this film within the college environment –

but what about festivals, or if it does end up being broadcast? You never know. It would make more sense, if you are at college, to find out if there are any musicians who would play for you, or if you know of a music college, to approach them with a project.

The sound editor will need to mix together the layers of sound, to make the final soundtrack for the film. If you are doing the sound mix yourself, there is some very basic information to get right about mixing sound. Have the dialogue in mono, keeping the sound central (don't pan left or right on the desk). As industry standard you will need some reference tone set at -18 dB (1 kHz tone) held for 1 minute at the front of your soundtrack. If you are recording digitally remember that digital sound is far less forgiving than analogue. Never get up as far as 0 dB with your sound – it will sound horrible!

Once you've finished the recording, transfer it onto a DAT (digital audio tape). It will need a one-frame 'sync pop' (a one-frame burst of tone at 1k) two seconds or 50 frames before the first frame of visuals, including the titles. Put another sync pop two seconds after the last frame as well. The editor should put a corresponding 'flash (white) frame' in exactly the same place on the picture.

And finally, you need to put on the credits. Be aware in what environment your film may be screened. Don't make the type too small either for big screen or for TV. If you want rolling credits, work on your instinct for a timing, neither too fast nor too slow. Don't let the credits end up as long as your film. There will be people who have contributed to your film, who it is very important to credit; check you have credited all funding agencies, all in-kind support and that any music is given a title and credit.

chapter 13

getting the job –
the business of animation

<table>
<tr>
<td>

**chapter
summary**

</td>
<td>

- *know your limitations*
- *different work, different studios*
- *commercials*
- *series*
- *TV specials and features*
- *applying for jobs*
- *your showreel*
- *festivals*
- *sending proposals to commissioning editors*

</td>
</tr>
</table>

My first experiments in animation were in my first year of art school. It was an assigned project, and after my first test shots, I knew this was for me. It seemed to be the perfect mix of art; sculpture, painting, lighting, performance and music. From then on I had a fairly clear path to follow. After two years in art school I moved to California to go to film school. I never had any training in character animation. I just interpreted my film assignments in animation, extremely crude, misinformed, uneducated stop motion. It was fun and I loved it, but the films were total crap. After I graduated I heard they were doing The New Adventures of Gumby in San Francisco. It was perfect, low-end entry level stop motion. So I moved to San Francisco to beg for a job, and eventually, they let me in. That's where I met a lot of the animators that I have worked with through the years, and that's where I learned how to animate.

Trey Thomas, animated Sally in *Nightmare Before Christmas*
and *James and the Giant Peach*

know your limitations

Many animation courses leave you unprepared for the business side of animation, concentrating more on giving you the experience of developing your ideas. When the likes of Jeff Newitt and Trey Thomas started out, an animation student was a rare thing. Nowadays, there are hundreds of animation courses. You may think that having done a three-year animation course, that you are an animator and ready to start work in a studio. This is of course possible, but there is a great difference between the type of work done at an art college and the sort of work that people make a living out of. In some rare cases a graduate will hit the market with just the right idea at the right time and have their work spotted at a festival or a degree show by a company representative. But for most of us there is a more circuitous route and it involves developing an understanding of what studios do and what they may be looking for by watching programmes, reading journals and trawling through websites.

different work, different studios

All studios have different reasons for their existence. Some are set up by animators trying to make their own films, but in order to sustain their work they may need to take on commercials from time to time. Others produce a steady stream of children's TV series. Very generally speaking, the UK animation industry struggles to survive in a market-driven system that means that often the only way the general public, other than small children, will get to see good British animation is in a commercial.

The UK does produce more animation than other European countries. In the past the French have had more luck with government subsidies and their television stations have had to follow a quota system that meant they had to show a majority of French work, but that seems to be changing now as funding becomes scarcer. American 2D animation is still the most popular, watched worldwide. However, the animation is kept to a limited style by budgets, and it tends to be dialogue/narrative driven.

The pre-school audience seems to be where model animation makes the biggest impression, especially in the UK. Its tactile, dimensional nature is what makes it so successful in marketing to a younger audience. In the US Clokey Productions make Gumby while in the UK, HOT Animation makes the very popular Bob the Builder and Cosgrove Hall Films produce a large number of the UK's children's TV programmes including remakes of popular classics such as Andy Pandy and Bill and Ben, and their own creations, Fetch the Vet and Engie Benjy.

commercials

Commercials are the jam on top for many animation teams. This is what the studios hope will pay the overheads and the wages for what is usually a skeleton staff. If all goes well they can salt away a little, and it may be used for projects that could expand the studio's repertoire.

With the kind of budgets sometimes available for commercial work, one would expect the benefits to be the high production qualities, innovative ideas and a chance to display one's talents. This is not always the case however, as the costs of the production can sometimes spiral in the decision-making process – and the results may not be quite the showcase one was expecting.

Loose Moose are a London-based animation company, mainly involved in commercials. Their clients include KP McVities, Kraft Foods, Energizer Batteries and Pepsi Lipton. The commercials they are best known for are Peperami (seen in the UK) and Brisk Tea (for the US; Figure 13.1). The team consists of two animation directors, Ken Lidster and Ange Palethorpe, two CGI animators, the producer Glenn Holberton, a production assistant, and a marketing manager.

In the first stage of the process, the client will choose an agency with a good track record. The agency will invite various animation companies to pitch for the job, sending round a script and a storyboard. Companies can invest a lot of time, effort and creativity just pitching for a commercial – developing characters and set designs and filming sometimes quite complex animatics. Ange Palethorpe, describes the process:

> When we pitch a job, we cost up all the character designs, and sets, crew and post production. Once we've got the job, there's generally 4 to 5 weeks of going back and forth to the client, checking characters. Then the Plasticine sculpts have to be approved by the client.
>
> The puppets are so expensive; all aspects have to be approved before being made in to real puppets. Something like the Brisk Tea ads will take longer as there are so many characters involved. We usually use Mackinnon & Saunders for puppets and Artem (a London company) for sets.

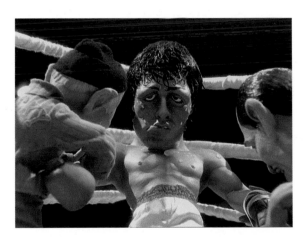

Figure 13.1 Still from *Rocky*. Courtesy Loose Moose Productions. © Brisk Tea/JWT

Based in the West End of London, a large studio space would be prohibitively expensive, so Loose Moose hire the space and the crew. Working in this way, they can rely on the professionalism of a team of experts, but as it's a hired space, they can't afford the luxury of testing time, unless there is a particularly generous budget. So the animators have to be prepared to go in and start 'cold'.

On a commercial Loose Moose shoot on average about 3 seconds of animation a day and shoot for about 10 to 15 days. If there is a chance, they will set up two units for a seven-day shoot.

By contrast **Aardman Animations** has most of its production on site. Even though they will hire in freelancers, they have a core of staff animators, a camera department, model making department and administrators. One of Aardman's creative directors, Luis Cook, describes his approach and the relationship between animation company and agency:

> As a creative director you need to know exactly what is going on around you, go to exhibitions, watch TV ads, look at hoardings, magazines. It may be art, it may be fashion, you might not like it – but you've got to be aware of it.

> When a job comes in I try and make it look as different as I can. Partly because it makes life more interesting for me and hopefully you don't get too stuck in a style. The idea always comes from the script and listening to who your client is – tonally. Which way they want to go with it? Is it going to be dark, is it going to be serious, is it going to funny, is it going to be brightly coloured, is it going to be fast-cutting, or slow? D'you want to make it boring? D'you want to make it exciting? All these things come from the script. D'you want to make it minimal or overloaded with imagery? Sometimes it's really obvious, other times you have to work at it and coax people round.

> You can only trust what the agency tell you, the client wants one thing, the agency another – it would be useful sometimes to go straight to the client, but you can't. You have to trust what the agency tells you. You have to remain calm if the agency goes wobbly. If they're coming at you with a terrible idea say 'hmm that's interesting. Let me have a think about it and get back to you' to give yourself space!

> On a recent commercial this American guy from the agency said to me 'This is a million dollar campaign, get rid of the art!' Culturally we were coming from different backgrounds, for him my ideas were too abstract. But, he was right – it became a very successful campaign and they shifted a lot of product!

series

Series work is often defined by its quick turnaround, lower budget nature. The characters are often refined down to a simple stylized design; the animation is also simplified, for greater speed and efficiency. It's very often these elements that make this form of animation so popular with children, and the same elements that give the characters marketable appeal. This in turn can make the medium a hot property for the TV companies and licensees.

Bob the Builder is a good example of a popular pre-school children's series. The studio, HOT Animation, was set up five years ago to produce this series and four half-hours of Brambly Hedge for HIT Entertainment. As Jackie Cockle, producer/managing director who runs training courses alongside the studio work, explains:

When I first started HOT, I didn't want to be part of the battle with other studios for freelance animators, I wanted to grow my own. We started out with two experienced animators and we took on 5 trainees on our scholarship course for 12 weeks and those animators went straight into production, so then we had our first seven. That's how we built the company up. It's only now that we're starting to use the odd freelance for holiday cover. We've trained up 15, and not lost any. They all do different characters and get involved in research and development. A lot are experienced prop-makers, in 'refurb' periods (between shoots, the puppets will be refurbished at Mackinnon & Saunders) they work on props or make flying rigs. In our company, runners usually go into editing or rigging work rather than go on to animate.

The animation is shot on a Bolex RX16 converted to Super 16mm, preferred by the US as it resolves well in High Definition.

You're striving each time to be better than the last, sustaining the creativity, the designs – we've done over 100 episodes now. It's character driven and we try to keep the characters growing and interacting all the time.

Series work sometimes gets put down as being a poor relation to specials and features. In fact it deserves applause because it's such hard work, you need a crew that's dedicated and efficient. It's like a little army getting down to work. We have week by week planned, we can tell you exactly what stage the production will be on a certain day. If your sets and your puppets and your costumes aren't ready, you're sunk.

Series work is one of the best training grounds for animation. Some of this country's best animators, Loyd Price, Paul Berry, Barry Purves, all developed their talent working for several years on programmes like *Wind in the Willows*, *Chorlton and the Wheelies* and *Cockleshell Bay* at Cosgrove Hall, a company who have produced 21 years of children's series for television.

TV specials and features

Probably the most challenging task for any animation team is a feature film. A half-hour TV special is a wonderful experience for animators in terms of handling continuity, and character development, but making a feature film tests the cohesion of a team in many ways. A feature film requires a huge team and soaks up anyone with animation skills for a long period. Often a graduate's first experience on a feature is being on a production line making one small part of a puppet, or cleaning up the same puppets over and over again ready for the next scene. This can be dispiriting, especially if you never get to see the rest of the studio. It takes all the company's resources to sustain in the crew a sense of following through a big adventure, and belief in the ultimate goal.

Working on Chicken Run was a much more fast and efficient way of animation. Before I was into refining movement and detail. Chicken Run was about making it work. The puppets were not really designed for refined animation, and yet that was what we were asking of them. A lot of the work was struggling with the puppets. Because clay is not really conducive to refined animation, but they asked an incredible preciseness, they pushed us far beyond anything I've ever done – it was the hardest thing I've ever done I think. As far as subtlety of emotion and subtlety of expression, Nick pushed us far beyond anything I've done before, maybe beyond anything that's ever been done, with claymation.

Guionne Leroy

Moving up one notch from being an animator to directing a team of animators can be a difficult transition.

Barry Purves reflects on directing *Hamilton Mattress*, a BBC Christmas Special made by Harvest Films:

On Hamilton Mattress I was directing four to five animators. The difficult thing is keeping an overall style and they were four very different animators. You have to allow them their creativity, so that when one makes Hamilton do something extraordinary, you have to let the other animators take elements of that. In trying to get a walk similar, an animator can be so focussed on that scene; he may forget how it fits in to the rest of the story. So I try to keep them all on track. When I'm the director and animator if I see a gesture going wrong, I can work my way out of it. Or if there's a cut point coming up – and I realise I'm just not going to be able to do it in time, then I can find something else to make it work. But directing animators, you are one step removed. It was hard trying to pull it all together, but the rewards are amazing, especially when some of them do something you just wouldn't have thought of.

Nick Park of Aardman Animations comments:

Working with a small team is quite easy. I still stayed very much in touch with the Plasticine myself on Wrong Trousers. We (Nick and Steve Box) did roughly half the animation each, but even on Wrong Trousers, I didn't want to let go of Wallace and Gromit, so Steve did all of the penguin. By Close Shave I did let go of it. Doing the animation of Wallace was the main risk: he might get a different shaped face – because we were manipulating his mouth in such a big, radical way it would be easy for the individual animator to put his own stamp on it and take it off in another direction. On A Close Shave we developed pre-made 'replacement' mouths for Wallace. We used it on Chicken Run, where each character had their own set of mouths. It helped keep it all consistent in style.

But each film I had to step back more. I say stepping back – it's not really stepping back, I did do a few scenes of my own in Close Shave – so I did feel I kept some hand on it – but on Chicken Run I couldn't animate. I never felt I'd lost control. There is a part of it I regret, because I do like doing the animation, I love doing it, but at the same time, to make a film of that size you can't afford to do that, because you have to spend your time going round telling everybody what to do. It is easier to do it yourself than to tell everybody else what to do!

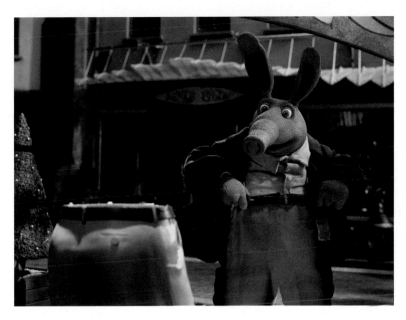

Figure 13.2 Courtesy of Harvest Films. © Hamilton Mattress 2002

As great as our animators were on Chicken Run, I think by the mere fact that a lot of people are working on it, the style can get homogenised, because everyone's trying to aim at a common thing. It's much harder to keep the edge on the style.

applying for jobs

When I got to college (Middlesex Poly) there suddenly was the facility, all I needed, 16mm gear just hanging around, Steenbecks, dubbing. So I started making films. I was making 3D as soon as I could, using Plasticine. I rang up FilmFair (a London company) and managed to get in there while I was still at College. They were doing Paddington Bear and I got involved making props. The college course was so unstructured that I was able to do 2 days a week at Film Fair. I then took all the bits I'd done there back to college and ended up with a very good showreel, with finished films rather than tests. In 1985 I finished college and went back to work at Film Fair and within a few months I was co-directing a series.

Jeff Newitt

He makes it sound so easy. These were different times – and Jeff, let's face it, is an exceptional talent.

Getting work with an animation company is more often than not a question of luck and timing – being in the right place at the right time. To improve your chances of being in the right place at the right time research the kind of work the companies do. Read industry magazines like *Campaign, Televisual, Creative Review, Cinefex.* Get a copy of *Animation*

UK: it's a directory with almost every animation company listed in it as well as TV companies, distributors, festival information – invaluable. Most companies now have a website which will tell you if they are looking for any particular skills. As a freelancer you need to be flexible and able to take a variety of different styles of direction. You also need to be prepared to relocate or work away from home.

Try and get a studio tour or a day observing or shadowing an animator. A good way in is to get work experience in a company. Ring the company and ask the receptionist first if they take on people for work experience and then ask who would be the best person to talk to. You have to be lucky, but if, once you are in, you show the right qualities: keen, quiet, good humoured, interested but not nosy, react quickly and ask good questions – you may get asked back. Remember when talking to the receptionist, they have the power to stop you right there – that is the person you must be nice to!

Degree shows are important – the better colleges mail out to invite production companies to degree shows. And the companies come if they can. Make sure your college does this.

your showreel

If you want to send your work in to try and get a job, it's important to follow a few basic rules otherwise no one will see your work.

- Label it. Sounds obvious, but we've all seen reels that once had a cardboard case and now are a blank VHS, or CD. Label the tape itself as well as the case with the title, your name, contact number and email address.
- Put your best work at the front. This could either be a quick compilation, or a short. There is no point in sending a long tape with examples of all of your work – unless your tutor or mentor advises it. But if your piece of work is very long, and the best bit's in the middle, edit! Give the viewer a 30-second trailer. Because if they haven't seen what they want in that time, they'll probably eject it.
- For the big companies, like Aardman or Cosgrove Hall in the UK or Vinton or Tippett Studios in the US, you should be prepared to wait for some time for a response. Usually they will view the work, then if it arouses interest, it'll go further and maybe be viewed by a director. *If they want you, they'll call you.* But the bigger companies get many showreels in every week and can't always get to look at them immediately, especially after graduation time. You may have to wait for between 2 and 3 months for a response; then if you've not heard anything, you could ring and ask for constructive comments. If you are sending work to the US from the UK, remember it must be an NTSC conversion, that's their standard – and for tapes coming to the UK from the US, a PAL conversion is needed.
- Another important point with your showreel is to clearly identify the pieces **you** have worked on and in what capacity. It's no good sending in a clip from something like *Chicken Run* on an animation showreel, when the truth is you were refurbishing parts in the model making department. Be honest and clear.
- Update your showreel every six months.

When you are making up business cards put an image from your film on it. This helps people see immediately what you do, and fixes your work in their mind.

Be reasonable about how you classify yourself – 'Joe Bloggs, Animator' sounds better than 'Joe Bloggs, Animator, Designer, Director, Illustrator'. The latter sounds like you don't have particular skills or ambition and will take any old job, this might be true but it doesn't instil confidence!

festivals

Try to keep your work seen – festivals are a growing business, there are more and more small festivals looking for different things.

The British Council (www.britcoun.org) list all the festivals and what the festivals are looking to screen, when their deadlines are. They can help with travelling expenses if your work is being screened abroad.

Be sure you know what formats are required for viewing, i.e. don't send a CD if they request VHS viewing copies.

sending proposals to commissioning editors

The job of a commissioning editor is to find the right programmes for a TV company. They have to find an idea that they believe in enough to be able to convince their own company as well as others. So this is what they need to know about your project:

1. **What is it about?**
   Send them two lines that encapsulate the whole idea. And a one-page synopsis of the proposal. That is what most commissioning editors want to see at first. They don't want pages and pages of script, or descriptions of merchandising opportunities. The idea is everything – the rest comes later.
2. **What will it look like?**
   Send some designs for your characters and some key visuals that display the style of the film. Don't send in original work, as this makes the recipient very nervous! No-one wants to be responsible for losing your work. So send in copies.
3. **What sort of audience will it attract?**
   Are you aiming this at children or adults? TV companies have very specific age group targets – look at channels to see how the programming changes throughout the day. Is your idea going to appeal to pre-school (1–4 yr olds); 5–7 yr olds; 8–10, 11 ,12? Children change very quickly through these ages. If it is an adult idea – how much animation do you see that is purely for adults? They do have to consider their market, and a really strange and obscure idea may not help them attract viewers.
4. **What slots on TV will it fit into?**
   Commissioning editors would all expect anyone approaching them with an idea to know what sort of format they are looking for – to have an understanding of which slots they can programme animation into.
5. **What's the duration?**
   Give them a story that fits their slots. Some will have slots for 5 or 10 minute animations, more common is the 26-minute series, in fact 13 × 26 is a favourite – so can you see your idea developing into 13 episodes?

6. **Is there anything similar already on TV or in production?**
   The commissioning editor needs to be aware that this idea is not going to be too like anything else that's coming on air. It sometimes happens that an idea becomes popular, several people seem to come up with the same idea – don't get paranoid, it doesn't necessarily mean that your work is being ripped off, it just means that you have your finger on the pulse and have created something of the moment – it happens.

Make your presentation look good. Handwriting can be charming but honestly it is better to have your stuff typewritten with a good layout – and no spelling mistakes.

You have to do everything to accommodate people who look at several scripts per day and, however dedicated they are to getting animation on TV, don't have all the time in the world to talk on the phone and to dwell over long scripts. If they are interested from your initial approach, they will invite you for a meeting, and if still interested they would probably draw up some sort of formal development agreement. You should get some legal advice of your own at this stage. The next stage would be for them to commission you to write the script. After that they would start to move on to looking at a production and budgeting – then you may be on your way . . .

Even if a commissioner wants your idea they may not be able to fully finance it. The majority of TV channels are not able to fully finance any project and will take a project to other companies for co-financing. They may take it to somewhere like the Cartoon Forum – this is a marketplace for work, set up by Cartoon, the European Association for Animated Film, an organization based in Belgium. It takes place in a different location in Europe each year and is attended by over 250 potential investors, all interested in animation. So it can be a *very* slow process from script to screen.

Commissioning an idea doesn't necessarily mean they want you to write it. An animator who can write their own material as well as direct and animate is a rare being (Peter Peake who directed *Pib and Pog* and *Humdrum* is one exception). It is likely that the producer would bring in a writing team or a script editor to work on your idea.

Be aware that what starts out as a personal project may end up being a very different, very public experience due to the nature of production and the sheer amount of people that become involved. It's like letting your baby grow up – don't be too precious – let it go into the wide world.

Lastly, there is a growing volume of work being done on computer. For all the horror stories I've heard about model animators being dragged kicking and screaming into the world of CGI, there are plenty of other success stories. Many successful model animators have made the transition to work in CGI and can move between the disciplines comfortably. Keep up your computer skills; in quiet periods between jobs, train up on new software, always keep on your toes and be aware of what's going on around you. But remember that animation skills are what is important – not software skills. Software will change, animation timing and performance are fundamental to all animation.

The last word goes to Jeff Newitt who has given me some great quotes to use in this book:

> *It's always a dress rehearsal – the public think you can hone it and hone it, but you can't – you only get one go. With a play like Hamlet, you know the story, you have the sets and the costumes – and you rehearse it. With animation its just 'You're on! There's the audience and there's the camera. Go!'*

bibliography

essential reading reference

The Animator's Survival Kit, by Richard Williams, Faber and Faber Ltd, 2001
The Human Figure in Motion, by Eadweard Muybridge, Dover Publications, 1989
Animals in Motion, by Eadweard Muybridge, Dover Publications, 1957
Timing for Animation, by Harold Whitaker and John Halas, Focal Press, 1981
The Illusion of Life, by Frank Thomas and Ollie Johnson, Hyperion, 1997
Cracking Animation, by Peter Lord and Brian Sibley, Thames & Hudson Ltd, London, 1998

definitely worth a look

How to Draw Cartoon Animation, by Preston Blair. Walter Foster Publishing, 1980
Tim Burton's Nightmare Before Christmas: The Film, the Art, the Vision, by Frank Thompson, Disney Press, 2002
Time-Lapse and Stop-Motion Animation using the Bolex H16, by Andrew Alden, www.bolex.co.uk
Film Fantasy Scrapbook, by Ray Harryhausen, Titan Books, 1989
Stop-Motion Armature Machining: A Construction Manual, by Tom Brierton, Jefferson, NC: McFarland & Company, Inc. 2002.

some old yet valuable information

Basic TV Staging, by Gerald Millerson, Focal Press, 1974
Motion Picture Camera Techniques, by David W. Samuelson, Focal Press, 1978

articles

Sight and Sound, no. 11, March 1992, pp. 24–7
The Same Dark Drift by Jonathan Romney
On the Brothers Quay

American Cinematographer, vol. 81, no. 8, Aug 2000, pp. 56, 62–65
Flying the Coop by John Gainsborough
On the making of 'Chicken Run'

Cinefex, no. 82, July 2000, pp. 119–31
Poultry in Motion by Kevin H. Martin
On the making of 'Chicken Run'

Cinfefex, no. 56, Nov 1993, pp. 30–53
Animation in the Third Dimension by Mark Cotta Vaz
On the making of Tim Burton's 'Nightmare before Christmas'

Creative Screenwriting, vol. 6, no. 6, Nov/Dec 1999, pp. 66–68
Writing for the Simpsons

Animation World Magazine, March 2000
Performance and Acting for Animators by Judy Lieff

software, camera and recording equipment suppliers

frame capture computer software

BTV Pro
www.bensoftware.com
Mac animation software

Framethief
www.framethief.com
Mac compatible

Stop Motion Pro
admin@stopmotionpro.com
PC compatible

DPS Reality
software/hardware
computer film services
Romans Business Park, Unit 9
East Street
Farnham
Surrey
GU9 7SX
t: 00 44(0)1252 718300
e: sales.europe@dps.com
www.dps.com

EOS
Eos House
Feidr Castell Business Park
Fishguard
Pembrokeshire
Wales
t: 00 44 (0)1446 741212
e: elin@eos-av.demon.co.uk

Computer Film Services
Peter Holland
Unit 66b York Road
Weybridge
Surrey
KT13 9DY
t: 00 44 (0)1932 850034
e: enquiries@computerfilm.com

LunchBox Sync™
Howard Mozeico
Animation Toolworks, Inc
t: 01 503-625-6438
f: 01 503-925-0221
e: howardm@animationtoolworks.com
www.animationtoolworks.com

sound

www.thirdwishsoftware.com

MagPie Pro

www.shure.com
microphones and general sound advice

film

Bernard Hunter/Bristol Ciné Sales
246 North Street
Bedminster
Bristol
BS3 1JD
t: 0117 966 6066
f: 0117 966 3139
e: cineman@aavon.com
www.aavoncom/bristolcine
recycling ciné equipment and film

Pro8mm UK
1–6 Falconberg Court
London
W1D 3AB
t: 0207 439 7008
e: giles@pro8mm2.com

Pro8mm US
2805 W. Magnolia Blvd
Burbank
CA 91505
t: 01 0 818 848 5522
e: sales@pro8mm.com
8mm equipment for sale and hire, film and
processing

The Widescreen Centre
Specialists Super 8
48 Dorset Street
London
W1H 3FH
t: 0171 935 2580

The Widescreen Centre
18 Lady Bay Road
West Bridgford
Nottingham
NG2 5BJ
t: 0115 945 5459

16mm

Andrew Alden
e: andrewalden1@btopenworld.com
www.bolex.co.uk
deals in second-hand equipment
see Bibliography

Bolex International SA
15 Route de Lausanne
CH – 1400
Yverdon-les-Bains
Switzerland
t: 00 41 24 425 60 21
f: 00 41 24 425 68 71
e: sales@bolex.ch
www.bolex.ch

Chambless Ciné Equipment
13368 Chatsworth Hwy
Ellijay, GA
30540-0231 USA
t: (706) 636 5210
f: (706) 636 5211 (24hr)
e: bolexcce@ellijay.com
specialize in Bolex cameras

www.ebay.com
Second-hand ciné equipment

Exclusive Film & Video
50 Portland St
Toronto
Ontario M5V 2M7
Canada
t: 416-598-2700

Visual Products, Inc.
790 Shiloh Avenue
Wellington, OH
44090 USA
t: 440-647-4999
f: 440-647-4998

35mm

Fries Engineering
8125 Lankershim Blvd
North Hollywood, CA
91605-1612 USA
t: 01 0 818-252-7700
f: 01 0 818-252-7709
e: info@frieseng.com
webmaster@frieseng.com
custom design cameras, motors and
directors finders

lighting

Arri Lighting Rental Ltd
20a Airlinks
Spitfire Way
Heston
Hounslow
Middlesex
TW5 9NR
www.arri.com

DHA Lighting Ltd
284–302 Waterloo Road
London
SE1 8RQ
t: 020 7771 2900
f: 020 7771 2901
ISDN: 020 7401 9202
e: sales@dhalighting.co.uk

Stage Electrics
Customer service team
Third Way
Avonmouth
Bristol
BS11 9YL
t: 0117 938 4000
f: 0117 916 2828
e: hire@stage-electrics.co.uk
e: sales@stage-electrics.co.uk

film services

Deluxe London
North Orbital Road
Denham
Uxbridge
Middlesex
UB9 5HQ
t: 00 44 (0)1895 832323
www.bydeluxe.com

Fuji Processing
Fujifilm House
125 Finchley Rd
London
NW3 6JH
www.fujifilm.co.uk/motion/index.html
Fuji photo film, motion picture and
professional video

Kodak Ltd
Station Road
Hemel Hempstead
Herts
HP1 IJU
t: 01442 261122
www.kodak.com/go/motionpicture
professional motion imaging

Kodak Processing
PO Box 2
Deer Park Road
Wimbledon
London
SW19 3UG

Pro8mm UK
1–6 Falconberg Court
London
W1D 3AB
t: 0207 439 7008
e: giles@pro8mm2.com

Pro8mm US
2805 W. Magnolia Blvd
Burbank, CA
91505 USA
t: 01 0 818 848 5522
e: sales@pro8mm.com
8mm equipment for sale and hire, film and
processing

Technicolor Film Services Ltd
Bath Road
West Drayton
Middlesex
UB7 0DB
t: 020 8759 5432

manufacturers and outlets

modelling clays

Art Studio Clay Co.
t: 00 1 800 323 0212
stockists of Ultracal

New Clay Products Ltd
1 Battle Road
Heathfield Industrial Estate
Newton Abbott
TQ12 6RY
t: 01626 835700
suppliers of modelling clays including
Newplast & Harbutt's Plasticine

Van Aken Plastilina
Van Aken International
9157 Rochester Court
Rancho Cucamonga
California 91729
USA
t: 909 850616
f: 909 980 2333

wire

Woolton Wire
4 Longworth Way
Liverpool
L25 6JJ
t: 0151 428 5097
f: 0151 421 0907
specialist suppliers of aluminium armature
wire for sculpture and model making
Suppliers of wire in the US:
www.mcmaster.com

sculpting tools etc

Alec Tiranti Ltd
High Street
Theale
Reading
RG7 5AR
www.tiranti.co.uk

Bath Potters Supplies
2 Dorset Close
Bath
BA2 3RF
t: 01225 337046

Burman Industries
14141 Covello Street, Suite 10c
Van Nuys, CA
91405 USA
t: 00 1 818 782 9833
f: 00 1 818 782 2863
instruction tapes on mold-making,
sculpting and painting

Hewlett Hind
Shrewton House
Shrewton
Salisbury
SP3 4HJ
t: 01980 620233

moulding materials

Alchemie
Warwick Road
Kineton

Warwick
CV35 0HU
t: 01926 641600
suppliers of silicones and resin

Bentley Chemicals
Rowland Way
Hoo Farm Industrial Estate
Kidderminster
Worcestershire
DY11 7RA
t: 01562 515121
suppliers of silicones, resins and various
modelling materials

Jacobson's Chemicals
The Crossways
Churt, Farnham
Surrey
GU10 2JD
t: 01428 713637
supply specialist silicones for moulding
and casting, Alginate, latex, Plastiline,
Sculpey, resin and most modelling
materials

Matrix Mouldings
Unit 8, Central Trading Estate
Bath Road
Brislington
Bristol
BS4 3EH
t: 0117 9715145
supply Jacobsons products and a variety of
resin, silicone and fibreglass materials

Mouldlife
Packhorse End
Bridge Street
Moulton
Newmarket
Suffolk
CB8 8SP
t:01638 750679
suppliers of silicones and moulding
materials

Sherman Laboratories
17 Tomswood Road
Chigwell
Essex
1G7 5QP
t: 0208 5591942
supplies good foam latex kits

South Western Industrial Plasters
63 Netherstreet
Bromham
Chippenham
SN15 2DP
t: 01380 850616
suppliers of plasters, silicones, latex, resin
and wet clay. Also supply modelling tools
and equipment

Thomas & Vines Ltd
Units 5 & 6
Sutherland Court
Moor Park Industrial Centre
Tolpits Lane
Watford
Herts
WD1 8SP
t: 01923 775111
www.flocking.co.uk

Burman Industries
14141 Covello Street, Suite 10c
Van Nuys, CA
91405 USA
t: 00 1 818 782 9833
f: 00 1 818 782 2863

The Monster Makers
7305 Detroit Ave
Cleveland, Ohio
44102 USA
t: 216-651-SPFX (7739)
f: 216-631-4FAX (4329)
e: sales@monstermakers.com
http://www.monstermakers.com
sole suppliers of McLaughlin Foam Latex

GM Foam, Inc.
14956 Delano St
Van Nuys, CA
91411 USA
t: 00 1 818 908 1087
f: 00 1 818-908 1262
www.Gmfoam.com

inks and paints

Paint Specialities Lab
www.graphiclynx.com/pslab

Sun Chemical Gibbon Inks and Coatings
25 Deer Park Road
Wimbledon
London
SW19 3UE
t: 020 8540 8531
f: 020 8542 5256

designers and modelmakers

Mackinnon & Saunders Ltd
148 Seamons Road
Altrincham
Cheshire
t: 0161 929 4441
f: 0161 929 1441
e: info@mackinnonandsaunders.com
www.mackinnonandsaunders.com

ScaryCat Studio
Gary Jackson and Cat Russ
77 Sandholme Road
Brislington
Bristol
BS4 3RX
t: 0117 9834060 or 01225 872872
e: mail@scarycatstudio.com
www.scarycatstudio.com

Stop Motion Works
Lionel Ivan Orozco
PO Box 2059
Daly City, CA
94017-2059 USA
t: 00 1 415-824-6888
e: stopmoworks@yahoo.com
www.geocities.com/stopmoworks

model-making supplies

EMA Model Supplies
Unit 2 Shepperton Business Park
Govett Avenue
Shepperton
TW17 8BA
t: 01932 228 228
f: 01932 253766
e: emashep@aol.com

armatures/ball and socket joints

UK

Gryphyn
716 Halifax Rd
Eastwood
Todmorden
Lancashire
OL14 6DP
t: 01706 818863
e: eduwe@easynet.co.uk

John Wright Modelmaking
Studio 1
Centrespace
6 Leonard's Lane
Bristol
BS1 1EA
t: 0117 9272854
e: mail@jwmm.co.uk
www.jwmm.co.uk
models props, armatures, set building

USA

Sherline Products, Inc
San Marcos
California
USA
t: 00 1 800 541 0735
manufactures miniature lathes and mill
column attachments

Stop Motion Works
t: 00 1 415 824 6888
e: stopmoworks@yahoo.com

magnets

Magnet Applications
North Bridge Road
Berkhampstead
Hertfordshire
HP4 1EH
t: 01442 875081
e: tracie_heffernan@magnetuk.com

Magnet Sales and Service Ltd
Unit 31
Blackworth Industrial Estate
Highworth
SN6 7NA
t: 01793 862100
f: 01793 862101
e: sales@magnetsales.co.uk

rigging

Climpex
S Murray and Co
Holborn House
Old Woking
Surrey
GU22 9LB
t: 01483 740099
f: 01483 755111
e: sales@smurray.co.uk

health and safety

Nederman Ltd
PO Box 503
91 Walton Summit
Bamber Bridge
Preston
Lancashire
PR5 8AF
supply health and safety equipment

appendix 3

calendar of animation festivals and film festivals incorporating animation

Sources:
British Council: www.britfilms.com
Animation World Network: www.awn.com/festivals
ASIFA, International Animated Film Association: www.asifa.net

january

Taiwan/Taipei

Golden Lion International Student Film Festival
Deadline: November
Awards: Golden Lion award (US $5000), Silver Lion award (US $3000), Bronze Lion award (US $2000), Special Jury award (US $5000), Audience award
Contact: Golden Lion International Student Film Festival, Motion Picture Dept., NTUA, 59, Da Kuan Rd., Sec. 1, Pun Chiao, Taipei County 220, Taiwan
t: (886 2) 2272 2181 x 358
f: (886 2) 2968 7563
e: d22@mail.ntua.edu.tw
www.ntua.edu.tw/~glion

UK/Middlesborough

Animex Student Animation Awards
Deadline: August
Contact: University of Teeside, Middlesborough, Tees Valley, TS1 3BA
www.animex.net

february

Spain/lleida

ANIMAC – International Animation Film Festival
Deadline: October
Awards: Non-competitive
Contact: International Animation Film Festival (ANIMAC), C/Major, 31, 25007 Lleida, Spain
t: (34 973) 700 325
f: (34 973) 700 325

e: animac@animac.info
www.animac.info

UK/Exeter

Animated Exeter
Deadline: November
Contact: Catherine Bailes, City Arts officer, Exeter City Council, Civic Centre, Paris Street, Exeter EX1 1JJ
t: 01392 265210
f: 01392 265366
e: catherine.bailes@exeter.gov.uk
www.animatedexeter.co.uk

february/march

Belgium

Anima – Brussels Cartoon and Animation Film Festival
Deadline: October
Contact: Folioscope/Anima 2003, Avenue de Stalingrad, 52, B–1000 Brussels, Belgium
t: (32 2) 534 4125
f: (32 2) 534 2279
e: info@folioscope.be
www.awn.com/folioscope/festival

USA/Miami

Miami International Film Festival
Deadline: September
Awards: Best Feature, Best Documentary, Best Short Film and Audience Award
Contact: Miami International Film Festival, FIU, University Park PC 230, Miami, Florida 33199, USA
t: (1 305) 348 5555
f: (1 305) 348 7055
e: info@miamifilmfestival.com
www.miamifilmfestival.com

march

Australia/Melbourne

Melbourne International Animation Festival
Deadline: December
Contact: The Melbourne Animation Festival, PO Box 1024, Collingwood, Melbourne, Victoria 3066, Australia
t: (61 3) 9416 4199
f: (61 3) 9419 1404
e: posseteam@hotmail.com
www.miaf.net

Finland/Tampere

Tampere International Short Film Festival
Deadline: December
Awards: International jury to award Grand Prix, a 'Kiss' trophy, for best film in the competition; three prizes for the best film in each category; one special prize; diplomas of merit and cash prizes awarded by the festival organizers
Contact: Tampere Film Festival, PO Box 305, 33101 Tampere, Finland
t: (358 3) 3146 6149
f: (358 3) 223 0121
e: office@tamperefilmfestival.fi
www.tamperefilmfestival.fi

UK/Belfast

Belfast Film Festival
Deadline: December
Awards: Non-competitive
Contact: Belfast Film Festival, Unit 18, North Street Arcade, Belfast BT1 1PB, United Kingdom
t: (44 28) 9032 5913
f: (44 28) 9032 5911
e: info@belfastfilmfestival.org
www.belfastfilmfestival.org

Germany/Stuttgart

Stuttgart International Animated Film Festival – Trickfilm Festival
(biennial; even years)
Deadline: December
Awards: Prizes to the value of € 54,500. State Capital of Stuttgart prize (€ 7500), State of Baden-Wuertemberg prize (€ 7500), international prize for best film (€ 15,000), Television audience prize (€ 12,000). Further prizes
Contact: Internationales Trickfilm-Festival, Stuttgart e.V, Teckstrasse 56 (Kulturpark Berg), D-70190 Stuttgart, Germany
t: (49 711) 925 4610
f: (49 711) 925 4615
e: Info@itfs.de
www.itfs.de

april

Italy/Positano

Cartoons on the Bay – International Festival & Conference on Television Animation
Deadline: January
Awards: Various
Contact: Cartoons on the Bay, International Festival and Conference on Television Animation, via U. Novaro, 18, 00195 Roma, Italia
t: (39 06) 37 498 315/423

f: (39 06) 37 515 631
e: cartoonsbay@raitrade.it
www.cartoonsbay.com

Norway/Oslo

Oslo Animation Film Festival
Deadline: January
Awards: Best film, Best debut, Best use of animation in commercial, Jury Special prize, Audience prize
Contact: Oslo Animation Film Festival, PB 867 Sentrum, 0104 Oslo, Norway
t: (47 23) 6930 0934

Germany/Dresden

Filmfest Dresden – International Festival for Animation and Short Films
Deadline: January
Awards: International Competition with awards totalling €22,000; National Competition with awards totalling €15,000
Contact: Filmfest Dresden, Alaunstr.62, 01099 Dresden, Germany
t: (49 351) 82947-0
f: (49 351) 82947-19
e: info@filmfest-dresden.de
www.filmfest-dresden.de

UK/Bristol

Animated Encounters – Bristol Animation Film Festival
Deadline: Contact festival for details
Awards: Contact festival for details
Contact: Animated Encounters, Watershed Media Centre, 1 Canon Road, Harbourside, Bristol BS1 5TX, United Kingdom
t: (44 117) 927 5102
f: (44 117) 930 9967
e: info@animated-encounters.org.uk
www.animated-encounters.org.uk

USA/Philadelphia

Philadelphia Film Festival
Deadline: January
Awards: Jury and audience awards, festival awards in several categories, including artistic achievement to directors and actors
Contact: Philadelphia Film Festival, c/o Philadelphia Film Society, 234 Market St, Fifth Floor, Philadelphia, PA 19147, USA
t: (1 215) 733 0608, ext. 237
f: (1 215) 733 0637
e: rmurray@tlavideo.com
www.phillyfests.com

USA/San Diego

San Diego International Film Festival
Deadline: February
Awards: Competitive for various categories
Contact: SDIFF, Dept 0078, UEO, 9500 Gilman Drive, La Jolla, CA 92093-0078, USA
t: (1 858) 822 3100
f: (1 858) 534 7665
e: rbaily@ucsd.edu
www.sdiff.com

april/may

USA/San Francisco

San Francisco International Film Festival
Deadline: November
Categories: Narrative features, documentaries, shorts, animation,
Awards: Golden Gate Awards for documentaries and shorts, cash prizes for various categories
Contact: San Francisco Film Society, 39 Mesa Street, Suite 110, The Presidio, San Francisco CA 94129, USA
t: (1 415) 561 5011/ 561 5014
f: (1 415) 561 5099
e: gga@sffs.org
www.sffs.org

USA/New York

Brooklyn International Film Festival
Deadline: October
Awards: Grand Chameleon award for the best film of the year, Chameleon Statuette award to the best film in each category
Contact: Brooklyn International Film Festival, 180 South 4th Street, Suite 2 South, Brooklyn, New York 11211, USA
t: (1 718) 388 4306/ 486 8181
f: (1 718) 599 5039
e: films@wbff.org
www.brooklynfilmfestival.org

may

Czech Republic/Zlin

International Film Festival for Children and Youth
Deadline: March
Awards: Various, including a 'Golden Slipper' for best film
Contact: Filmfest, s.r.o., Filmova 174 , 761 79 Zlin, Czech Republic
t: (420 577) 592 441, 592 300
f: (420 577) 592 442

e: festival@in-zlin.cz
www.in-zlin.cz

may/june

France/Annecy

Festival International du Film d'Animation
(plus film market)
Deadline: January
Awards: Grand Prize for best animated film, two special distinction prizes and a special distinction prize for best computer-animated film. Also prizes for fiction films (shorts and feature films), for commissioned and television films, and for internet animation
Contact: Festival International du Film d'Animation, 6 Ave des Iles, BP 399, 74013 Annecy Cedex, France
t: (33 4) 5010 0900
f: (33 4) 5010 0970
e: info@annecy.org
www.annecy.org

june

Russia/St Petersburg

Message To Man – St Petersburg International Film Festival
Deadline: April
Awards: Grand Prix: Golden Centaur plus US $5000. Four other cash awards of US$2000 each for best feature documentary, best short documentary, best short, best animation. Also cash awards for best debut films
Contact: Message to Man Film Festival, 12 Karavannaya Street, 191011 St Petersburg, Russia
t: (7 812) 230 2200/235 2660
f: (7 812) 235 3995/235 2660
e: info@message-to-man.spb.ru
www.message-to-man.spb.ru

Croatia/Zagreb

Zagreb World Festival of Animated Films
(biennial; even years)
Deadline: February
Awards: Money award for the Grand Prize and for the first film. Awards for three best student films.
Contact: World Festival of Animated Films, Animafest, Kneza Mislava 18, 10000 Zagreb, Croatia
t: (385 1) 450 1190
f: (385 1) 461 1808
e: animafest@kdz.hr
www. animafest.hr

july

Brazil/Rio de Janeiro

Anima Mundi – International Animation Festival of Brazil
Deadline: April
Awards: Audience award (trophy and cash) and professional jury award (trophy and cash)
Contact: Anima Mundi, c/o Iman Imagens Animadas Ltda, Rua Elvira Machado 7, casa 5, 22280-060 RJ Botafogo, Rio de Janeiro, Brazil
t: (55 21) 2543 7499
f: (55 21) 2543 8860
e: info@animamundi.com.br
www.animamundi.com.br

Ireland/Galway

Galway Film Fleadh
Deadline: April
Awards: Audience award, best first feature, best Irish short
Contact: Galway Film Fleadh, Cluain Mhuire, Monivea Road, Galway, Republic of Ireland
t: (353 91) 751 655
f: (353 91) 735 831
e: gaflead@iol.ie
www.galwayfilmfleadh.com

Tanzania/Zanzibar

Festival of The Dhow Countries
Deadline: May
Awards: Golden Dhow and Silver Dhow
Administrative address: Festival of The Dhow Countries, Box 3032, Zanzibar, Tanzania
t: (255 4) 747 411 499
f: (255 4) 747 419 955
e: ziff@ziff.or.tz
www.ziff.or.tz

august

Japan/Hiroshima

International Animation Festival
(biennial; even years)
Deadline: March
Awards: Grand Prix (¥1 million), Hiroshima prize (¥1 million), début prize (¥500,000), Renzo Kinoshita Prize (¥250,000) Special International Jury Prize(s), Prize(s) for outstanding works
Contact: Hiroshima Festival Office, 4–17 Kako-machi, Naka-ku, Hiroshima 730-0812, Japan
t: (81 82) 245 0245
f: (81 82) 245 0246

e: hiroanim@urban.ne.jp
www.urban.ne.jp/home/hiroanim

UK/Edinburgh

Edinburgh International Film Festival
Deadline: April
Awards: Awards include: McLaren award for new British animation, Michael Powell award for best new British feature
Contact: Edinburgh International Film Festival, Filmhouse, 88 Lothian Road, Edinburgh EH3 9BZ, United Kingdom
t: (44 131) 228 4051
f: (44 131) 229 5501
e: info@edfilmfest.org.uk
www.edfilmfest.org.uk

USA/Palm Springs

Palm Springs International Festival of Short Films
Deadline: May
Awards: Cash and merit awards in all categories
Contact: Palm Springs International Film Festival, 1700 East Tahquitz Canyon Way, Suite 3, Palm Springs, CA 92262 USA
t: (1 760) 322 2930
f: (1 760) 322 4087
e: info@psfilmfest.org
www.psfilmfest.org

USA/Los Angeles

World Animation Celebration
Deadline: June
Awards: Competitive. Prizes in various categories
Contact: World Animation Celebration, 30101 Agoura Court, Suite 110, Agoura Hills, CA 91301, USA
t: (1 818) 575 9615
f: (1 818) 575 9620
e: info@wacfest.com
Director: Dan Bolton
www.wacfest.com/mission.html

september

USA/New York

New York Animation Festival
Deadline: May
Awards: Competitive
Contact: New York Animation Festival, PO Box 1513, New York, NY 10009, USA

t: (1 212) 479 7742
e: info@nyaf.org
www.nyaf.org

september/october

Ukraine/Kiev

KROK International Animation Festival
Deadline: May
Awards: Competitive
Administrative address: KROK International Animation Festival, Saksaganskogo St. 6, 01033 Kiev, Ukraine
t: (380 44) 227 5280/ 227 6629
f: (380 44) 227 3130
e: krok2001@ukr.net

october

Canada/Ottawa

Ottawa International Student Animation Festival
Deadline: June
Awards: Competitive
Contact: Ottawa International Student Animation Festival, c/o Canadian Film Institute, 2 Daly Avenue, Ottawa, Ontario K1N 6E2, Canada
t: (1 613) 232 8769
f: (1 613) 232 6315
e: oiaf@ottawa.com
www.awn.com/ottawa

Ottawa International Animation Festival
(biennial; even years)
Deadline: July
Awards: Competitive. Various awards in different categories.
Contact: Ottawa International Animation Festival, c/o Canadian Film Institute, 2 Daly Avenue, Ottawa, Ontario K1N 6E2, Canada
t: (1 613) 232 8769
f: (1 613) 232 6315
e: info@animationfestival.ca
www.awn.com/ottawa

France/Bourg en Bresse

Festival of Animation for Young People
(biennial; even years)
Deadline: April
Awards: Main prize in each category from an international jury and an official young people's jury

Festival and administrative address: Festival du Film d'Animation pour la Jeunesse, Maison des Sociétés, Immeuble Chambard, Boulevard Joliot Curie, 01000 Bourg en Bresse, France
t: (33 4) 7423 6039
f: (33 4) 7424 8280
e: festival-bourg@wanadoo.fr

Australia/Brisbane

Brisbane International Animation Festival
Deadline: August
Awards: Various awards. Contact festival for further details.
Contact: Brisbane International Animation Festival, PO Box 8266, Woolloongabba Qld 4102, Australia
t: (61 7) 3229 1112
f: (61 7) 3220 0359
e: info@biaf.com.au
www.biaf.com.au

Germany/Wiesbaden

Wiesbaden International Weekend of Animation
Deadline: Contact festival for details
Contact: Wiesbaden International Weekend of Animation, Freunde der Filme im Schloss, Klopstockstr. 12, D-65187 Wiesbaden, Germany
t: (49 611) 840 562
f: (49 611) 807 985
e: info@filme-im-schloss.de
www.filme-im-schloss.de

Germany/Leipzig

Leipzig International Festival for Documentary and Animated Films
Deadline: August
by dialogue script in German, Russian, English, French or Spanish
Awards: Several cash prizes in various categories
Contact: Dokfestival Leipzig, Große Fleischergasse 11, 04109 Leipzig, Germany
t: (49 341) 980 3921
f: (49 341) 980 6141
e: info@dokfestival-leipzig.de
www.dokfestival-leipzig.de

Slovakia/Bratislava

Biennial Animation Festival – Bratislava
(biennial; odd years)
Deadline: June
Awards: Various awards
Administrative address: Biennial Animation Festival, Bratislava, Bibiana, Panská 41, 814 99 Bratislava, Slovakia

t: (421 2) 544 31 314
f: (421 2) 544 31 314
e: bab@bibiana.sk

South Africa/Durban

The Durban International Film Festival
Deadline: June
Awards: Various awards
Administrative address: The Durban International Film Festival, Centre for Creative Arts, University of Natal, Durban, 4041, South Africa
t: (27 31) 260 2506
f: (27 31) 260 3074
e: diff@nu.ac.za
www.und.ac.za/und/carts

Sweden/Uppsala

Uppsala International Short Film Festival
Deadline: July
Awards: Uppsala Grand Prix, Special Prizes of the Jury, Audience Award
Contact: Uppsala International Short Film Festival, Box 1746, SE-751 47 Uppsala, Sweden
t: (46 18) 120 025
f: (46 18) 121 350
e: uppsala@shortfilmfestival.com
www.shortfilmfestival.com

UK/Norwich

FAN International Animation Festival
(biennial; odd years)
Deadline: June
Awards: Best International Animation, Best International Student Animation, Best Independent Animation, Best Commercial Animation, Best Animated Pop Promo, Best Experimental Animation, Best UK Student Animation and The Cinewomen Award for the best animation by a female director in any category
Contact: FAN International Animation Festival, Norwich School of Art & Design, St George Street, Norwich NR3 1BB, United Kingdom
t: (44 1603) 610 561
f: (44 1603) 615 728
e: r.hanna@nsad.ac.uk
www.filmartsnorwich.co.uk

UK/Leeds

Leeds International Film Festival
Deadline: July
Awards: Competitive
Contact: Leeds International Film Festival, Town Hall, The Headrow, Leeds LS1 3AD, United Kingdom

t: (44 113) 247 8398
f: (44 113) 247 8494
e: filmfestival@leeds.gov.uk
www.leedsfilm.com

november

Netherlands/Utrecht

Holland Animation Film Festival
Deadline: September
Awards: Grand Prix for best film or video. Prizes in each category
Contact: Holland Animation Film Festival, Hoogt 4, 3512 GW Utrecht, Netherlands
t: (31 30) 2331733
f: (31 30) 2331079
e: info@haff.nl
www.awn.com/haff

Portugal/Espinho

Cinanima Espinho International Animation Film Festival
Deadline: July
Awards: A single award in each of the categories
Festival and administrative address: Organizing Committee, Cinanima, Rua 62, 251, Apartado 743, 4500-901 Espinho Codex, Portugal
t: (351 22) 733 1350/1
f: (351 22) 733 1358
e: cinanima@mail.telepac.pt
www.cinanima.pt

Slovenia/Ljubljana

Ljubljana International Film Festival
Deadline: September
Awards: Kingfisher Award (€ 5000) − perspective section
Contact: Ljubljana International Film Festival, Cankarjev Dom, Presernova 10, 1000 Ljubljana, Slovenia
t: (386 1) 241 71 47/50
f: (386 1) 241 72 98
e: jelka.stergel@cd-cc.si, info@cd-cc.si
www.ljubljanafilmfestival.org

South Africa/Johannesburg

South African International Film Festival
Deadline: July
Awards: Non-competitive, except for a short films competition for Southern African film-makers

Contact: South African International Film Festival, PO Box 32362, Bloemfontein 2017, South Africa
t: (27 11) 403 2541/403 3436
f: (27 11) 403 1025

Spain/Barcelona

L'Alternativa – Barcelona Independent Film Festival
Deadline: July
Awards: One in each major category
Contact: L'Alternativa – Barcelona Independent Film Festival, Centre de Cultura Contemporanea de Barcelona, C/Montalegre 5, 08001 Barcelona, Spain
t: (34 93) 306 4100
f: (34 93) 301 8251
e: alternativa@cccb.org
alternativa.cccb.org

Spain/Bilbao

Bilbao International Festival of Documentary and Short Films
Deadline: September
Awards: Grand Prix €6010; Gold Mikeldi €3005; Silver Mikeldi €1803
Contact: MªAngeles Olea, Festival of Documentary and Short Film, Colón de Larreátegui 37-4 Dcha, 48009 Bilbao, Spain
t: (34 94) 4245507/4248698
f: (34 94) 4245624

UK/Bradford

Bradford Animation Festival (BAF!)
Deadline: July
Awards: Competitive
Contact: National Museum of Photography, Film & Television, Bradford BD1 1NQ, United Kingdom
t: (44 1274) 203 308
f: (44 1274) 394 540
e: a.pugh@nmsi.ac.uk
www.baf.org.uk

november/december

Turkey/Ankara

Ankara International Film Festival
Deadline: August
Awards: Various awards, contact festival for more information
Contact: Ankara International Film Festival, Farabi sok. No. 29, 1 Cankaya, Ankara, Turkey
t: (90 312) 468 7745

f: (90 312) 467 7830
e: festival@filmfestankara.org.tr
www.filmfestankara.org.tr

december
USA/Anchorage

Anchorage Film Festival
Deadline: September
Awards: Various cash prizes, contact festival for further details
Contact: Anchorage Film Festival, 1410 Rudakof Circle, Anchorage, AK 99508, USA
t: (1 907) 338 3690
f: (1 907) 338 3857
e: filmsak@alaska.net
www.anchoragefilmfestival.com

animation courses that include or specialize in stop motion and related organizations and websites

This list is not comprehensive, but the organizations and websites I have included in this appendix will help any further searches. Courses marked with ETNA are members of the European Training Network for Animation – see page 199.

Australia

Victorian College of the Arts
234 St Kilda Road
Southbank
Victoria 3006
Australia
Contact: Michelle van Kampen
t: 61 3 9685 9000
f: 61 3 9685 9001
e: m.vankampen@vca.unimelb.edu.au
www.vca.unimelb.edu.au
A one year Graduate Diploma course open to mature age students with previous experience or degree level education in animation, art and communication related disciplines. School of Film and Television

Belgium

La Cambre
Hogeschool, section Animation
21 Abbaye de La Cambre
1000 Bruxelles
Belgium
t: 32 2 648 96 19
f: +32 2 640 96 93
e: lacambre@lacambre.be
www.lacambre.be

Canada

Cégep du Vieux Montreal
Département d'Animation
255, rue Ontario Est
Montréal, Quebec H2X 1X6
t: 514 982 3437
f: 514 982 3448
e: gestionnairew3@cvm.qc.ca
http://cgi.cvm.qc.ca/cours/EnseignementOrdinaire/programmes/574_A0.htm
http://cgi.cvm.qc.ca/cours/EnseignementOrdinaire/programmes/574_B0.htm
Coordinator: Pierre Grenier
Traditional animation to back up computer animation training

Sheridan College
Centre for Animation and Emerging Technology
1430 Trafalgar Road
Oakville
Ontario
L6H 2L1
t: 905 845 9430
e: infosheridan@sheridanc.on.ca
www.sheridanc.on.ca/learning/schools.html

Vancouver Institute of Media Arts (VanArts)
837 Beatty St
Vancouver, BC V6B 2M6
t: 604-682-2787 or 1-800-396-2787
e: ken@vanarts.com
www.vanarts.com
Admissions Manager/Animation Instructor: Ken Priebe
Part-time courses in stop motion

Denmark

The Animation Workshop (ETNA)
Will run stop motion classes when there is demand
L1 Skt Hans Gade
8800 Viborg
Denmark
Contacts: Morten Thorning and Søren Fleng
Storyboard and layout for series and feature films (twice 2 weeks)
Character animation (twice 14 weeks and once 2 weeks)

France

L'Ecole des Métiers du Cinema d'Animation (ETNA)
1, Rue de la Charente
1600 Angoulême
France

t: 33 (5) 45 93 60 70
f: 33 (5) 45 93 60 80
e: lleguen@angouleme.cci.fr
Contacts: Loïc Le Guen and Christian Arnau

La Poudrière, Ecole du Film d'Animation (ETNA)
12, rue Jean Bertin
26000 Valence
France
t: 33 (4) 75 82 08 08
f: 33 (4) 75 82 08 07
e: poudriere@wanadoo.fr
Contact: Isabelle Elzière-Delalle
Directing animation film: creative and artistic aspects (2 year course)

Spain

Centro Integral de Cursos Especializados (CICE)
Maldonado 48
Madrid, 28006
Spain
t: 34 (91) 401 07 02
e: cice@cicesa.com
www.cicesa.com
www.cicesa.com/diseno/formacion/c cortometrajes.html
Contact: Marco Antonio Fernandez Doldan
Computer animation with traditional training in stop motion

Fak d'Art (ETNA)
Muntaner 401, entlo
8021 Barcelona
España
t: 34 (93) 201 08 55
e: fbenavent@fda.es
Contacts: Fransisco Benavent and Jordi Martorell
New technologies applied to traditional animation: pre-production (4 months), post-production (4 months)

UK

Arts Institute at Bournemouth
Wallisdown
Poole
BH12 5HH
t: 44 (0) 1202 533011
f: 44 (0) 1202 537729
e: general@arts-inst-bournemouth.ac.uk
www.arts-inst-bournemouth.ac.uk

Programme Director: Peter Parr
BA (Hons) Film and Animation Production. Three-year course enabling students to develop specialization and skills necessary for their chosen career

Edinburgh College of Art
BA (Hons) Visual Communication – Animation
Lauriston Place
Edinburgh
EH3 9DF
t: 44 (0)131 221 6000
e: d.holwill@eca.ac.uk
Head of Animation: Donald Holwill

Glamorgan Centre for Art and Design Technology
Glyntaff Road
Glyntaff
Pontypridd
CF37 4AT
t: 44 (0) 1443 663309
e: artcol@pontypridd.ac.uk
Award Leader: Peter Hodges
HND and BA(Hons) Animation

National Film and Television School
Beaconsfield Studios
Station Road
Beaconsfield
Buckinghamshire
t: 01494 731425
e: admin@ftsfilm-tv.ac.uk
www.nftsfilm-tv.ac.uk
MA Animation Direction

Norwich School of Art and Design
St Georges Road
Norwich
Norfolk
NR3 1BB
t: 01603 610561
e: info@nsad.ac.uk
www.nsad.ac.uk
MA Animation and Sound Design

The Royal College of Art
Kensington Gore
London
SW7 2EU

t: 44 (0)20 7590 4500
e: info@rca.ac.uk
www.rca.ac.uk
Head of Animation: Professor Joan Ashworth
MA Animation

The University of the West of England

Bower Ashton Campus
Kennel Lodge Road
Bristol
BS3 2JT
t: 0117 966 0222/4707
f: 0117 344 4820
The Bristol Animation Courses **(ETNA)** *– 3-month courses for graduates*
BA (Hons) courses attached to graphic design, illustration and time-based media
MA Animation

University of Wales College, Newport

School of Art, Media and Design
Caeleon Campus
PO Box 179
Newport
South Wales
t: 01633 432182
e: caroline.parsons@newport.ac.uk
BA (Hons) Animation

USA

California Institute of the Arts

Program in Experimental Animation. BFA, MFA
School of Film/Video
24 700 McBean Parkway
Valencia, CA 91355-2397
t: 661 255 1050
f: 661 253 7824
e: admiss@calarts.edu
www.calarts.edu

The Douglas Education Center

Douglas Education Center
130 Seventh Street
Monessen, PA 15062
t: 724.684.3684
www.douglas-school.com
Rick Catizone's Art of Animation Diploma Program
16-month program designed to provide students with the skills necessary for a career in animation.

Art Institute of Pittsburgh
420 Boulevard of the Allies
Pittsburgh, PA 15219
t: 800 275 2470
f: 412 263 3715
e: admissions-aip@aii.edu
www.aip.aii.edu

Rhode Island School of Design
Film, animation, video
2 College St
Providence, RI 02903-2791
t: 401 454 6233
f: 401 454 6356
e: hhey@risd.edu
www.risd.edu

Rochester Institute of Technology
School of Film and Animation
Frank E. Gannett Building
70 Lomb Memorial Drive
Rochester, NY 14623-5604
t: 716 475 2754
f: 716 475 7575
e: animate@rit.edu
www.rit.edu/~animate
30 week program of stop motion skills

training – key organizations

UK

Organizations offering training in film-making and related areas in the UK. Apart from courses in full time education, many organizations offer professional, vocational training for freelancers.

Skillset
Skillset is the national training organization for broadcast, film, video and multimedia. The site includes careers advice for those wishing to get in to the industry and those already working. The site gives information about individual training courses and their scheme to fund 60% of vocational training on certain other courses. The Film Council give training funds to organizations to run courses, including through Skillset but *not* to individuals needing funding.
www.skillset.org

BECTU (Broadcasting, Entertainment, Cinematograph and Theatre Union)
This is the national training organization for broadcast, film, video and multimedia. The skills base part of the site includes a subsidized careers advice for those wishing to get in to the

industry and those already working. The site also gives information about individual training courses and their scheme to fund 60% of vocational training on certain other courses.
www.bectu.org.uk

METIER

Metier are the national training organization for the arts and entertainment industries including performance art, visual art, literary art, arts development and teaching, technical support and production design, arts management administration and support roles.
www.metier.org.uk

Europe

ETNA

The European Training Network for Animation includes eight European professional animation training centres as well as around 40 European animation studios. The goals of this network are to perfect European animation training, to encourage and better the links between animation training and industry requirements and developments, and to facilitate the mobility of European professionals throughout Europe.
www.cartoon-media.be

other useful organizations

CARTOON

European Association of Animation Film. Incorporates Cartoon Forum, Cartoon Masters, Cartoon d'Or, Cartoon Movie, Jobs and News
Timothy Leborgne
314, Boulevard Lambermont
1030 Brussels
Belgium
www.cartoon-media.be

ASIFA

International Animated Film Association/Association Internationale du Film d'Animation ASIFA was formed in 1960 by an international group of animators to co-ordinate, further the interests and increase world-wide visibility of animation. The Association is founded in the firm belief that the art of animation can be enriched and greatly developed through close international co-operation and the free exchange of ideas, experience and information between all who are concerned with animation. ASIFA's membership includes over 1500 animation professionals and fans in more than 50 countries.
http://asifa.net

Animation World Network

A website resource with jobs, directories, articles.
www.awn.com

Stopmotionanimation.com

Animator Anthony Scott's website for discussions on any subject to do with animation.

index

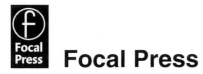
Focal Press

www.focalpress.com
Join Focal Press on-line
As a member you will enjoy the following benefits:

- an email bulletin with **information on new books**

- a regular **Focal Press Newsletter**:

    - featuring a selection of new titles

    - keeps you informed of **special offers, discounts and freebies**

    - alerts you to **Focal Press news and events** such as author signings and seminars

- complete access to **free content** and reference material on the focalpress site, such as the focalXtra articles and commentary from our authors

- a **Sneak Preview** of selected titles (sample chapters) *before* they publish

- a chance to have your say on our **discussion boards** and **review books** for other Focal readers

Focal Club Members are invited to give us feedback on our products and services.
Email: worldmarketing@focalpress.com – we want to hear your views!

Membership is **FREE**. To join, visit our website and register. If you require any further information regarding the on-line club please contact:

Lucy Lomas-Walker
Email: l.lomas@elsevier.com
Tel: +44 (0) 1865 314438
Fax: +44 (0)1865 314572
Address: Focal Press, Linacre House,
Jordan Hill, Oxford, UK, OX2 8DP

Catalogue
For information on all Focal Press titles, our full catalogue is available online at www.focalpress.com and all titles can be purchased here via secure online ordering, or contact us for a free printed version:

USA
Email: christine.degon@bhusa.com
Tel: +1 781 904 2607 T

Europe and rest of world
Email: j.blackford@elsevier.com
Tel: +44 (0)1865 314220

Potential authors
If you have an idea for a book, please get in touch:

USA
editors@focalpress.com

Europe and rest of world
focal.press@elsevier.com